Full Disclosure

STORMY DANIELS

WITH

KEVIN CARR O'LEARY

PAN BOOKS

First published 2018 by St Martin's Press, New York

First published in the UK 2018 by Macmillan

This paperback edition first published 2019 by Pan Books
an imprint of Pan Macmillan
20 New Wharf Road, London N1 9RR
Associated companies throughout the world
www.panmacmillan.com

ISBN 978-1-5290-1381-8

1 3 5 7 9 8 6 4 2

A CIP catalogue record for this book is available from the British Library.

Printed and bound by CPI Group (UK) Ltd, Croydon, CR0 4YY

Visit www.panmacmillan.com to read more about all our books
and to buy them. You will also find features, author interviews and
news of any author events, and you can sign up for e-newsletters
so that you're always first to hear about our new releases.

To my smart, brave, beautiful daughter.
You remind me every day what truly matters.

NOTE

From the moment I first met her, I knew Stormy Daniels was different. I've had the good fortune to meet a lot of people along the way from different walks of life—janitors, construction workers, hard-working blue-collar workers, middle managers, executives, working moms, homemakers, and CEOs. From people who were broke and down on their luck to billionaires who will never want for anything. But I've never met anyone quite like Stormy Daniels.

What makes Stormy Daniels so unique—and so prepared for the important role she has undertaken—is that she always owns who she is. She is entirely confident in her own skin—every day. She doesn't try to pretend to be something she isn't. Not even when sometimes I wish she would (see her Twitter account). In a day and age where image is everything and everyone is vying for that perfect Instagram pic or the ideal tweet, Stormy is . . . herself.

That is very refreshing. And it is something to be cherished.

Her journey so far has been an amazing one. And we don't know yet where it ends. My hope for this book is that it will let you learn who Stormy Daniels really is. I am confident that when you do, you will agree that we are all very lucky to have her.

—Michael Avenatti, Esq.

Full Disclosure

PROLOGUE

My phone buzzed again and again with friends texting me the same message: "Happy Stormy Daniels Day!" It was two o'clock, and I had two hours before the city of West Hollywood was set to give me the key to the city at an outdoor ceremony on Santa Monica Boulevard. Mayor John Duran had proclaimed May 23 to be Stormy Daniels Day, and yes, it seemed just as surreal to me as it did to everyone else.

I texted each friend back, sipping a Red Bull. My gay dads, Keith and JD, know to keep the house stocked with energy drinks when I come stay with them in L.A. And snacks. If you and I are going to be friends, we need an understanding that there must always be snacks involved. My two bodyguards, Brandon and Travis, pulled up to the house in an SUV. They have been at my side since the beginning of April, when the death threats against me and my family started ratcheting up, but I have never seen them nervous until that moment as they walked up to the house carrying a bag. I had given them a very important mission: go to Marciano to pick out a dress for me to wear to the ceremony. "I'm a small right now," I had told them, "but keep in mind I have big boobs."

To hedge their bets Brandon and Travis bought two dresses, in peach and black, and presented them to me for approval. I narrowed my eyes, because hazing the people I love is a favorite pastime, before saying quietly, "Guys, you did great! Bodyguards *and* stylists?" I went with the black one, a Capella cutout bandage dress which fit perfectly, and kept Thunder and Lightning— my nickname for my breasts—in check.

I think I put off buying a dress because I was so nervous about giving a speech. Because I am an adult film actress, director, and dancer, when I meet people they usually have some nagging question about what gives me the nerve to think I can do something. How do I do porn or take my clothes off onstage in clubs? Or take on the president of the United States? No, the thing that amazes me most about this past year is that I can speak in front of people. Because when I was a student at Scotlandville Magnet High School in my hometown of Baton Rouge, sure, I got straight As, but I always took a zero rather than talk in front of the class. My fear was so crippling, my voice so shaky, that I could not get out of my seat. The first time this happened was in ninth grade—an oral book report on *Little Women*. Of course, I read it—I read everything I could back then. And Jo March was the perfect character for me to talk about because, just like me, she wanted to be a writer. More than that, I identified with Jo's frustration with what the world was ready to allow a girl to do. And no, I did not think she should have married old Professor Bhaer. (Sorry if that is a spoiler, but if you narrowed your next read down to this one or *Little Women,* you need to examine your life choices.)

But I couldn't get my voice to come out. I took a straight-up F, and did so every time an assignment called for public speaking. I didn't want people looking at me. Judging me. Which is exactly what has happened ever since March, when I gave *60 Minutes* a free interview that was worth millions. It was important to me that I go to a reputable, impartial news source when I first set the record straight about Donald Trump's personal attorney repeatedly trying to get me to lie about a sexual encounter I had with the president in 2006. The interview covered what happened in a hotel room, and later, when my life was threatened in a parking lot. But it wasn't the full story—it didn't cover the "why" of my decisions and the real, personal costs to me. I was starring in films I wrote and directed in L.A., then going home to my suburban life with my husband and seven-year-old daughter in Texas. It's the life I dreamed of and worked hard to have, and I have to keep reminding myself that that life is over. For all I've lost, I deserve the chance to defend myself and state all the facts. That's why I chose to share what you are about to read.

I'm also doing this for all the people who have come to see me dance in my shows, waiting in longer and longer lines to take a photo with me and share a moment. I have been dancing in clubs since I was seventeen. As my fan base grew over two decades of work in film and feature dancing, my demographic was usually middle-aged white men. Forty-five- to sixty-five-year-old white dudes—Republicans, basically. I lost a lot of them, and that's their choice. This is, after all, America.

They were replaced and outnumbered by people of color, gay men, and lots and lots of white women in their forties. These are people who have never come to strip clubs before, and there's a learning curve to a strip club. My old crowd was well versed in the etiquette, thank you. If they specifically came to see me, it meant they were into adult entertainment, so they had likely been to a convention or at least seen another porn star at a strip club. They know how to act. They don't take pictures during the show, and they definitely don't grab me to tell me they love me. Because I'm in heels, and if a guy pulls me, I will fall. And a bouncer will throw him out, *Roadhouse* style.

If you're familiar with the term "New Money," you will understand the concept of New Strip Club Patron. And now my shows are full of them. The gay men seem to fall into two categories: the good-timers and the witnesses to history, and I love them both. I can't tell you how many times men from the former group have told me, "This is the first time we ever paid to get into a strip club—that has a vagina." A lot of them come with props for the meet-and-greet photos, like bags of Cheetos or a Make America Gay Again hat. The latter group of gay men is more emotional, and after the show they talk to me about feeling bullied by an administration that makes their marriages and freedoms seem less safe. Their fear is real, and when they confide in me, it comes from an authentic place. It was shared by my gay dads, the family I chose in my twenties when I gave up on my biological parents. Keith and JD were two of the only people who knew that I had a secret about Trump pre-election, and there was a time after the 2016 election when their concerns about their upcoming marriage turned into resentment of me for not coming forward and upending my life to save theirs.

I realized the women were coming out to see me when I started getting hurt Facebook messages from strangers some mornings after my shows. "We came to support you but they didn't let us in!" Packs of single women were coming to the clubs in groups of four or five, only to be turned away by bouncers. Normally, a straight woman can only come in the club if she is escorted by a man, because it's assumed that if she's solo she is looking for a husband or a sale. Now, I make sure the club owner knows they have to let women in.

The women I see on the road have a lot of anger. Not at me, which I initially expected. I was worried I wouldn't be safe anymore in clubs. No, they're angry at Trump, who seems to be a stand-in for every man who's ever bullied them. Nashville, Shreveport, Baltimore . . . "You have to get him," they say. "Get that orange turd." Many of these women are quieter as they wait in line to talk to me, then grip my arm to tell me about someone they didn't speak up for. A friend who killed herself after being raped. Or their own stories, feeling voiceless and unprotected. I stand there, a girl in a cute dress who just stripped onstage a few minutes before. These women transfer all the energy to me and leave feeling unburdened, but now it's mine to carry.

They leave me with "You're going to save the world." In April, a woman at a meet-and-greet upgraded my job to saving the universe. No pressure. It's these women who gut me, never the Twitter troll who calls me a slut or the guy in a crowd yelling "whore." I sometimes think my job in porn prepared me for all this, because you can call me any name in the book and I've heard it from some other judgy loser. But nothing in my life prepared me for the confidences and hopes of people who come to see me. Even though it's all positive energy, it's still all pointing at me. The best way I can describe it is going to the beach and being in the sun all day. It's great, but you feel sick when you get back to your room. In my case, it's absorbing it all until it hits some limit I didn't see coming, and I am suddenly on the floor of my hotel room, sobbing when no one can see me. I let myself feel it once, and then I get back up. I call it wringing out the sponge.

Besides, it was Stormy Daniels Day, and the hero had to show up and speak. Before I left, I FaceTimed with my daughter, who was home in Texas with the tutor we had to hire because it's impossible to send her to school and shield her from what everyone is saying about her mother. She was at a zoo with her tutor, and for ten minutes, I stopped everything to hang on every brilliant word of a seven-year-old's telling of her day's adventure.

"I can't wait to see you not digitally," she said.

"I'll see you Friday, baby," I said. "How many sleeps is that?"

"Two."

To avoid paparazzi taking pictures of our family, we've had to arrange meet-ups in other cities. People learned that if there was even a two-day gap in my schedule, I would be home with my girl in Texas. They camped out at the house and the stable where we ride. This time we'd be going to Miami, where at least she could swim with dolphins.

"Mommy loves you," I said.

And then my little traveling circus was off to the ceremony. When we got to Santa Monica Boulevard, there was a friends-and-family area inside Chi Chi LaRue's store. Keith and JD were inside, greeting everyone, in total hosting mode for their daughter's day. Mayor John Duran and Mayor Pro Tem John D'Amico arrived, followed by my lawyer, Michael Avenatti. As always, I smiled at how many people wanted a picture with him and how many people made excuses to touch his arm. An assistant to the mayor asked Michael if he'd like to speak, but you know how shy he is. Kidding—of course he said yes. As always, he offered to write my speech for me, and as always, I said no. Partly because I know it scares him, but mostly to make it mine.

A throng of people had shown up, and the floor-to-ceiling windows of the store gave it the feel of a fishbowl, with photographers and fans pressed against the roped-off speaking area outside. Brandon and Travis paced, already scoping for trouble in the crowd.

"You ready?" Michael asked me.

I nodded. The mayor, mayor pro tem, my gay dads, Michael, and my dragon bodyguards all crowded onto the tiny stage. "There's one thing I can promise about Stormy Daniels," Michael told the crowd. "And that is: She's not packing up; she's not going home. She will be in for the long fight, each and every day until it is concluded."

John D'Amico handed me the key to the city, and the girl who took a zero rather than be judged just started talking. "So, I'm not really sure what the key opens," I said. "I'm hoping it's the wine cellar. But in all seriousness, the city of West Hollywood is a truly special place, very close to my heart."

A man in the crowd started yelling, "How big is Trump?" *Keep going, Stormy,* I thought.

"As a woman with two wonderful gay dads, Keith and JD, I feel especially at home here. The community of West Hollywood was founded more than three decades ago on the principle that everyone should be treated with dignity and fairness and decency."

"How small is Trump?"

"And this community has a history of standing up to bullies and speaking truth to power. I'm so very, very lucky to be a part of it."

Back inside, I read the mayor's proclamation and I was again struck by the absurdity of my life. I should be living in a trailer back in Louisiana, with six kids and no teeth. I grew up in a house that I should never have escaped, with adults never coming to my aid. I started stripping in high school and still graduated with honors as editor of the school paper. I won the respect of a male-dominated industry as a screenwriter and director. And despite everything I did to stay out of it, I ended up in the middle of one of the biggest political scandals in American history.

I know that the deck has always been stacked against me, and there is absolutely no reason for me to have made it to where I am, right here talking to you. Except that maybe the universe loves an underdog as much as I do. I own my story and the choices I made. They may not be the ones you would have made, but I stand by them.

Here's my story. It has the added benefit of being true.

ONE

We watched as the tornado tore through the field of sunflowers.

It was a little skinny one, miles away from where my mom and I sat on the front steps of our building. North Dakota was so big and flat that you could sit in the bright sunshine and watch a storm blow through in the distance like a movie. This was late July, the summer we lived in a Bismarck apartment complex that looked to two-year-old me as if it had been pulled from *Sesame Street*. Our building was across from a sunflower farm, black and gold flowers facing east as far as you could see.

"Look at the twister," my mom kept saying. "Look at the twister."

I wasn't scared. I was never that kind of kid. I was the girl who walked home from the Little People Academy preschool when I was two. Just slipped out during naptime. "I don't nap," I told my mother when she answered the door. She sighed. I had confounded her since birth, when the boy she had planned and decorated a nursery for turned out to be a girl. She was inconsolable for a week. I was supposed to be called Stephan Andrew after a late relative, but she and I were stuck with Stephanie Ann. If we should ever meet, call me Stormy.

That summer of the tornado, my mom bought me black roller skates with red laces and red wheels. I just loved the look of them, but she was determined to teach me how to skate. She'd put me down on the concrete and hold her arms out. "Come here," she'd say. Sheila Gregory was beautiful then, a twenty-seven-year-old Julianne Moore look-alike with freckles and blue eyes. She wore her strawberry-blond hair long and straight, parted in the middle, a seventies look she successfully brought with her into 1981. She was short and thin, and people would say, "Aren't you a tiny thing?"

She seemed even smaller next to my dad. Bill Gregory is six foot four, with chiseled features and olive skin owed to Cherokee blood somewhere in the line. I am a perfect combination of Sheila and Bill, a mix that could have gone horribly wrong. I had tight, super curly blond hair, and I am smart like my dad. We traveled for his work as an architectural engineer, going to new water treatment plants to map out where the electricity should go. My mom was not what you'd call a big thinker. She'd never had a job in her life, and I can't recall her ever even picking up a book.

What my mom did care about was my father. They had a very passionate relationship, and she had a jealous redhead temper. She liked to throw things, though never at me. Just warning shots at him. She had had her pick of men and went on some dates with Kurt Russell when she was seventeen. She met him at the Louisiana State Capitol while she was with my grandmother, who had jury duty. Kurt was there shooting a movie, *The Deadly Tower*. He took one look at my mother and he was a smitten kitten. He asked her out and my grandparents let her go, but supervised. Even my grandmother would talk about the night Kurt Russell picked my mom up in a limo and they went to a fancy dinner. Then he didn't get anywhere because she was underage. They held hands, so that was the end of that.

Bismarck was just a quick stop for us. We kept a house in Baton Rouge, where I was born, and my father's parents lived next door so they could keep an eye on the place. But we were rarely there. Our Suburban was always packed up, and my dad had a matching boat, which went everywhere with us, no matter how landlocked the new place might be. Any chance he had to take it out for waterskiing, he took it. Otherwise, it was just a trailer. We'd load all our stuff in it, put the cover on, and drive to the next place.

I have a photographic memory, so I can put myself right back in every place we lived. There was Kissimmee, Florida, and the winter in Kalamazoo, which my mom hated. All she did was complain and smoke in the house because Michigan was too cold to go outside. After Bismarck we moved to Idaho Falls. We rented a house on Amy Lane, a tiny street dotted with spruces that looked like Christmas trees. We had a big beautiful backyard with a long concrete sidewalk leading to a barn that still had horse stalls. Somebody who lived there had kept horses, and I would sit in the cool of the barn, trying to summon the ghosts of these horses.

Mom made a friend, Nicky Fontenot, who I called Miss Nicky. She owned a horse named Prissy Puddin' and she barrel raced. One day I was at the stable, and Miss Nicky was cooling out the horse after racing. Prissy was sweaty and tired, and someone put me, all of two, up on the horse to sit in front of Miss

Nicky. I can remember the smell of the saddle and the horse sweat, her bay coat and black mane. It was magic, and I don't know a time since that I haven't wanted to ride.

I was an only child, and my mom made no secret about the fact that my father never wanted kids in the first place. I have always known that she got pregnant on purpose, and he tolerated the one. He was never bad to me, but he just didn't have that dad instinct. He barely acknowledged my existence, and I adored him.

So naturally, when I was four and needed to start school, there was no question about my father's lifestyle changing. It just wouldn't. My mom and I moved into the house in Baton Rouge, and he took a job in Alaska. For a while, he sent me stuffed animals from that region. My favorite was a little husky. Dad would take pictures from his job site, great big eight-by-tens of this desolate flat land and the arctic foxes he trained to come near him by feeding them fried chicken. "I almost have them eating out of my hand," he told me on the phone.

He wouldn't answer when I asked when he was coming home or when I could visit.

The house on Mcclelland Court was small, with a front yard that was two equal rectangles of blacktop driveway and patchy grass. The street was a part of a horseshoe-shaped development where every house had the same look and layout. We lived in a three-bedroom ranch-style house they had no business calling a three-bedroom. I had a waterbed tucked in a vinyl-covered frame, so I at least thought that was cool. The houses next door were just a few feet away from each other, and if you want to buy one of them today, the estimated going price is twenty-four thousand dollars.

My mom took me to a dance class because I wanted to be a ballerina. My dance teacher was Miss Vicki, and her crotchety old mother, Miss Donna, owned the studio. The recital that year had a Disney theme, and I can still see my costume: baby blue and fully sequined with a little ruffle on my butt. And white tights, white tap shoes, and a white sequined hat. What's funny is that I now have the same hat in black for when I play a magician when I do my feature dancing gigs in clubs on the road. Every time I put on the magician hat, I think back to that recital.

Backstage, it was full-on *Toddlers & Tiaras,* with all the Baton Rouge moms teasing out their daughters' hair. Everyone was smoking, and my mom was trying to secure my hat to my hair by bobby-pinning it directly to my skull. With all the hair spray and polyester, I was a pint-size fire hazard for sure.

"Ow," I screamed over and over as she pinned the hat on. "That hurts!"

Miss Donna hobbled over and shook a finger at me as she exhaled smoke. "You have to suffer to be beautiful," she rasped. *"Beauty is pain."*

Then she hobbled on, and I was speechless. But no truer words have ever been spoken. Little did I know the future would involve plucking and waxing. High heels, corsets, and underwires.

It was around then that I had my first boyfriend. Jason Beau Morgan lived next door to my mother's mother, who I called Mawmaw Red. We were dating because I said so, telling him in my grandmother's front yard, "You're my boyfriend." He had blue eyes and curly hair the color of light sand. I actually cut out a picture of his face and put it in a locket that I still have.

We lost touch after elementary school, and in middle school I heard he died of a brain aneurysm. Jason was the first boy I ever held hands with.

I was especially close to Mawmaw Red and loved visiting her, not just for the chance to play tag with Jason. She would give me café au lait—with extra milk and sugar in a tall, skinny brown plastic cup—and had blocks that she hid from her other grandkids. They were just for me to play with. "You are special, Stephanie," she would tell me in her Louisiana drawl.

Mawmaw Red had emphysema. When I went to her house in the last several months of her life, she wore an oxygen mask, and the big green tank went around the house with her until she just stayed in one room. I remember the smell of the oxygen, how it triggered memories of when we lived in Idaho and my asthma was so bad I had to be hospitalized in a crib with a bubble canopy. I pretended I was a fish in a bowl, until I got bored and decided to escape.

The August after my dad started work in Alaska, Mawmaw Red deteriorated, and my mom took me to the hospital to say good-bye. She couldn't talk and was so close to death. I remember thinking she looked like the death scene in *E.T.* "You must be dead," Elliott says to E.T. "'Cause I don't know how to feel. I can't feel anything anymore. You've gone someplace else now."

I spent the night at my father's parents' house next door, and the next day I was at home when my mom came into her room, where I was playing. I was standing by the bed and she sank down to her knees to take me by both arms.

"I have to tell you something," she said. "Mawmaw Red died." She was sobbing, so upset, but I wasn't sad. I was relieved.

Mawmaw's just gone someplace else now, I thought. My mom remained distraught in the days leading up to the funeral.

Dad came home to attend, and he decided that was a good time to tell her he was leaving her. He'd met someone else. I knew her name was Susan because, well, my mother was screaming about "that whore Susan." They sent me next door to my grandparents, but I still heard all the screaming and the sounds of plates smashing against walls as my mother went ballistic. Worse, he had brought Susan with him from Alaska, and while he was in town, my mom spotted them and tried to beat the shit out of her.

My mom was so caught up in her understandable grief that she didn't seem to remember I existed. She was just different, listless and uninterested in doing anything with me. The next thing I knew, the Suburban was backed into the driveway with the hatch up. My dad loaded it up, just like he did all the times we'd moved as a family, only it was just his stuff. I was aware he was leaving, and as my mom screamed at him for the whole neighborhood to hear, I played quietly in the patch of front yard.

When he went in to get one last thing, my mother chased him inside to continue yelling at him. This was my chance. I climbed in the Suburban and hid myself behind some boxes. Nobody noticed I was missing, and it has never occurred to me until I'm right here writing this that he didn't look for me to say good-bye. He just got in the Suburban, slammed the door, and drove off into his new life.

He got a couple of miles down the road when I decided the coast was clear and I could surprise him.

"Hi!" I said. I thought he would be happy. We were escaping together. Instead, he looked sad and pulled over.

"Baby, you can't stay," he said. "I gotta take you home."

"I don't wanna go home," I said. As he did a U-turn, I began to wail, hitting boxes and crying. I just knew home wasn't safe anymore. I have always had a good sense of things, and everything in me told me that I needed to run.

He had to pull me out of the car, and my mom screamed at both of us. She had to hold me in her grip and drag me into the house to keep me from running after the car. He married Susan, and he started his new life without me.

I didn't see my father again for almost three years.

My mother instantly became a different person, as if my father's leaving had triggered an Off switch. She drank Coca-Colas all day, lighting each new cigarette off the one she was just finishing, then stubbing it out in an ashtray or whatever was close. She didn't care what she looked like, and her hair became gray and got curly, seemingly overnight. Thirty years old and she had to go to work for the first time in her life. She got a waitressing job at a restaurant called Café Lagrange, and then a second job working at Tigator trucking company across the bridge in Port Allen, Louisiana. When the restaurant closed down, she took on more work at Tigator. They had a fleet of blaze-orange eighteen-wheelers, all with a logo of a two-headed animal that was part tiger, part alligator.

She had been a great mom, but now she paid less and less attention to me. Part of it was that she now had to work these minimum-wage jobs, but mostly I think my father just broke her heart. She quickly devolved, and a lot of people wondered if she was doing drugs or drinking. I wish she had been, because her actions would make more sense. I've seen my mom drunk maybe five times. On wine coolers at barbecues, places where it's perfectly appropriate to relax and do that.

My dad left and my mom never cleaned the house or even did dishes again. It was so gross, but it became just how I grew up. I am not a clean freak and I am not OCD. I can do so much damage cluttering up a hotel room in two days, you cannot imagine. But there is a difference between being messy—dumping my suitcase on the floor to find the one thing I cannot find—and being dirty. This was fucking dirty.

At least I could go next door to my grandparents' house for a little normalcy, but that ended when my grandmother passed away when I was six. My grandfather sold the house as quick as he could and moved to Mississippi. A couple moved in with a little boy named Travis. He was six months younger than me, and we became best friends.

Grandpa sold just in time. My mom and the neighborhood were in a race to see which could go downhill faster. The population of the neighborhood changed just as the crack epidemic hit Baton Rouge. What was once a stable, working-class neighborhood became a real-time loop of *Cops*. Even the yards gave up. The trees and lawns all died, and cars started getting parked in the yard.

Rats moved in, and their poop was all over the house. They loved the third bedroom, which became a literal junk room. They could have it. The real problem was roaches. They were everywhere in the house and no place was safe. I had a waterbed and I don't think my mother washed those sheets once after

Dad left. The roaches hid in it, waiting for me. I have scars on my legs from where they would bite me.

We had this toothbrush holder, a plastic teddy bear that had holes in his hands and feet to hold two kids' brushes. When it was new, you could pull a string and the bear's arms and legs moved as he blinked at you. But my toothbrush had outgrown it, and the teddy bear sat empty on the wall for the roaches to turn into another nest. I'd look in the holes and the roaches would just be in there, their antennae waving at me like, "Fuck you." It bothered me because I could remember when it was new and clean, when we had Dad around and I had a real mom.

There were many days I came home from school to no electricity. We were always getting shut off for nonpayment. I'd be home alone after school, the house getting darker as the sun got closer to setting. I wasn't scared, but I was bored and hungry. I'd go out and ride my bike, which wasn't really safe in the neighborhood, or go hang out at a friend's house. I had a lot of friends from school and the neighborhood, though in those days I never once had anyone over. "I'll come to your house," I'd say. "You guys have better snacks." Travis next door was always fun to play with. He taught me how to ride a bike, and we took turns with his. Who else was going to teach me?

Travis was great, but he wasn't a crush or anything like that. Back then I had eyes for Tanya Roberts in 1984's *Sheena*. I saw the movie on TV—a sort of female version of *Tarzan*—and I've never forgotten the thrill I felt watching her. She was perfection, a blonde with phenomenal boobs in a torn-up makeshift bikini. Tanya played an orphan raised by an African tribe, who can communicate with animals. What drew me in was that Sheena is as strong as she is pretty. She gets the bad guy by shooting him in the heart with an arrow, then saves the boyfriend and then sends him home to America so she can ride off *on a zebra*.

The hot girl who saves the day. Who wouldn't fall for her?

My dad remarried and I guess Susan, who I had still never met, suggested that maybe he should see his daughter. In the three years since I had tried to run away with him, they had moved to Philadelphia. I was six, and my dad wanted me to fly up by myself. There were a lot of screaming phone calls. My mom felt strongly that if he wanted to see me, he should come get me, and this is one of the rare cases where I was on her side. I was not an outgoing kid, so if I was lost or something happened, I would have just decided to live in the airport rather than ask an adult for help.

Susan flew down to Baton Rouge, but on reflection I think my father might have told my mom that he was coming and sent her instead. The last time my mom saw Susan she was dragging her around by the hair, and now she had to hand her daughter over to the woman who ran off with her husband. She referred to Susan as my Wicked Stepmother, and I think it pissed her off even more that Susan was so polite at the airport. We flew to Philadelphia, and I didn't talk very much until she brought me to my dad. I was so excited to see him.

He was exactly how he was before, a little distant and not at all hands-on. He was nice enough, but I don't think he had any idea what to make of me. Their town house wasn't a mansion, but to me it was. It was clean and didn't reek of smoke.

"The first thing we're gonna do is wash all these clothes," Susan said, recoiling from the stale smell of smoke as she unpacked my bag. She bought me a ton of new clothes and seemed way more excited about seeing me than my dad did. I actually spent very little time with him that week, except for when he took me to see the Liberty Bell. This was back when you could still touch it, and he held me up to reach my hand to the crack in the bell. I remember it so vividly, me in my pink jacket and pigtails, touching history.

I spent the week sleeping on their living room floor, right by a floor-to-ceiling glass window and a door that led to their back patio, which was like a mini yard. The window had huge vertical blinds, and one morning at about 5 A.M. I saw a shadow go across the ceiling. I crawled over and looked through the blinds. I so wish you could have seen this: There were bunnies everywhere. There were about twenty of them, all doing mating dances, leaping into the air and darting under each other like a goddamned bunny ballet. I thought, *Am I dreaming?*

Dad had to see this. I ran to their bedroom and woke him and Susan, and neither of them was impressed. "Go back to bed," my dad said.

After that week, they—and I'm sure it was just Susan—set up a schedule of visits. I'd go see them for a couple of weeks in the summer and then either around Christmas or Easter. All my birthday cards and Christmas cards came from her, with her signing his name for him. Every time I went to see them, it was like going to Narnia. Each visit started with washing my clothes. She was kind and set up art projects for us to do, but she was not pushy. She didn't want to play Mom for the week, and I wasn't looking for one. I wasn't searching for anything from my dad, either. I'd stowed away in his car and he'd brought me home. I can take a hint.

No, the trips weren't about him. This was a short period of time where I slept in a clean bed, there was food, and my asthma wasn't acting up from my mom's chain-smoking.

And then I'd go home.

After Dad, my mom dated this parade of horrible guys. It was like if someone mentioned a guy, her first question was "Is he a loser? Yeah? Sold." None of them came on to me, which I know is what people assume happened to adult actresses to "damage them" as children. No, they were just losers.

When I was about eight, my mom started disappearing for days at a time, probably with one of the guys she was dating. There would be no food, and I just wasn't sure how long I would have to ration out saltines or whatever was still there. When she was gone, I would watch TV until late. I loved late-night talk shows and the companionship of the last years of Johnny Carson on *The Tonight Show*. Saturday nights were best, because I could watch *Saturday Night Live*. Dana Carvey, Phil Hartman, Jan Hooks, Kevin Nealon—they became my heroes. The humor just clicked with me, the thrill that I was sitting there alone in Baton Rouge, and in that very second, they were making these jokes live from New York. All of us sharing this moment.

When my mother came home, she never offered an explanation or an apology. I didn't think she was capable of either. She wasn't off on a romantic getaway. She probably just went to hang out at a car garage where some guy worked, went home with him, and then he drove her to whatever job she was doing. And then when she needed a ride to her car . . . rinse and repeat. She also hung out at a bar called the Gold Dust Lounge. I just wasn't on her radar as a priority, and by the time I was eight she was used to treating me with less care than you would a dog.

There was one man, a big, heavy dude named Wade, who was so in love with her. Wade was a nice guy with a decent job, so she wasn't interested. But she did use him. He would come over after work and bring us groceries. Wade always sat in the easy chair by the big picture window. I couldn't understand why anyone would volunteer to be in the house. He didn't mind the rat poop and didn't seem disgusted by the roaches. He would ask me about school, which no one else did.

"It's good," I told him, meaning it. I had realized I was smart when I started finishing my work in class before everyone else. My friends complained about quizzes and I worried that I was missing something. At school I was a leader. Not in a *Mean Girls* kind of way, but when we played games or pretended we were wild horses galloping around, I was always the leader and no one ever questioned it. There was never anyone saying, "I'm gonna be the leader today." It was just natural that it be me.

It was natural to me, too. I always felt like there was some kind of magic around me. Maybe you could chalk it up to my having an exceptional imagination as a kid, but not all of it. There was a vibration that people picked up on. Like the universe had a plan for me.

By the end of fourth grade, I had found my first bad boy. Damien MacMorris was in my class, and his mom, Sharon, was friends with my mom. They lived in a mobile home in a trailer park. He had dark hair and dark eyes, and he was always, always in trouble. He was my boyfriend, though we'd never kissed.

His parents were divorced, and on the last day of school, he was going to live at his dad's. My mom and I were over at his place, and Sheila and Sharon chain-smoked in the trailer, probably talking about how men suck. I didn't know if Damien was leaving for the summer or for good, but I had a feeling this was the last time we were going to see each other.

The trailer park had concrete pads, and the spot next to his had no mobile home on it. We were sharpening sticks and using them to draw on the cement.

"I'm gonna miss you," I said.

He looked down and absently started singing Bon Jovi's "You Give Love a Bad Name." It was still on the radio all the time.

"Why are you singing that?" I asked.

"'Cause it reminds me of you," Damien said. "I'll think of you every time I hear it."

His mom poked her head out of the door. "Your dad's coming to get you in thirty minutes!" Sharon hollered. "Is all your stuff packed to go?"

"Yeah!" he yelled.

This horrible anxiety seized me, a feeling that I would never see him again. I dropped my stick, grabbed him by the arm, and pulled him behind a tree to kiss him. My very first time. I think in my rush, I missed the target and kissed him more on the side of the lips, but it didn't matter. It gave me the butterflies feeling of an orgasm. Like it was bad, and "What if our moms see us?"

We smiled at each other, both of us still surprised by what I'd done. I heard the wheels of a car pull up. It was his dad. Damien got in the car and I never saw him again.

I found out years later that he died—the rumor was that he was shot to death. He *was* bad. If you're keeping score, yes, number one and number two are dead. Fucking black widow.

Twenty years later, I was driving when "You Give Love a Bad

Name" came on the radio. I'd never really listened to the lyrics, and as I did my mind wandered back to that day when I kissed Damien. I nearly drove off the road when it got to the line, "Your very first kiss was your first kiss good-bye." Thanks for the memory, Damien.

When Damien moved away, I moved on to kissing my next great love, Patrick Swayze. I had a poster of him in my room because I loved him so much in *Dirty Dancing*. I kissed a hole in that poster. That movie is still my favorite, and I can still do every dance step. I was Baby for Halloween three years in a row as a kid. The real draw was Patrick, who I knew from an interview raised horses. I remember him saying he had two Straight Egyptian purebred Arabians, and four "fun horses" in California.

I was in Cincinnati visiting my dad in his new house and was probably talking about Patrick Swayze having horses when Susan interrupted me.

"You know," she said, "I grew up with horses."

"What?" I said. It was like she told me she was part fairy. She got out her scrapbook from when she was a kid in Palos Verdes, California. The best part was that she had clippings from her horse's mane in it. I touched it, thinking of Prissy Puddin', the horse I rode with Miss Nicky when I was two. The hair was still silky, but so strong.

"Her name was Tasine," Susan said. "We had her mother, Taffy, and the dad's name was Jacine." She showed me pictures of her riding English, so formal in her flat saddle with both hands on the reins. She had the breeches and boots, and a huge smile under her equestrian helmet. Seeing the photos, I realized that not only did I love horses, I loved that type of riding.

Susan was the first person sympathetic to that need to ride. Horse people can spot each other. The following year, when I was nine, she took me for my very first official English horseback riding lesson at Derbyshire Stables in Cincinnati. I rode a horse named Kiowa, and Susan bought me my first pair of riding boots. When I put them on, it was my Cinderella moment. I felt hot and powerful. They weren't even nice ones and looked cheap, but I didn't care. I was a horseback rider. After that, I pushed for more and more visits because I knew she would take me for lessons.

Back home, I rode my bike like I was on Kiowa, my territory extending around the horseshoe-shaped development of our neighborhood. One day I was out riding when I met a girl named Vanessa the way kids do, pausing to stare at each other until one says, "Do you wanna play?"

I dropped my bike as an answer, and we pretended we were horses in the pasture. I became best friends with Vanessa, whom I am still so protective of that I want to be up front with you and say that's not her real name. She was a year and a half younger than me, and sometimes the age difference showed enough that I felt like a big sister. Vanessa sometimes seemed even younger because she had a problem with wetting her pants. It happened every time she laughed, even when she had just gone to the bathroom. She was ashamed about it, and I would try to make it less of a big deal, pressing Pause on the playtime and helping her inside to change before her mom saw.

"You're okay," I would say, partly because I often felt responsible for the problem because I had made her laugh. It was easy to slip by her mom, since she had a bunch of kids crammed into a tiny house the same size as mine. In the summer she watched older kids, too. My mother had me go over there for the day, and I'm not sure if she paid Vanessa's mom anything or if she just figured I would be hanging out with Vanessa anyway.

One day when I was nine I rode my bike over and I couldn't find Vanessa. By then I could just walk into the house. Her mom was changing a diaper. "She's next door watching a movie," she said.

It was weird, because I didn't know a kid lived there. I'd only ever seen a guy in his forties, always home because he didn't seem to have a job. I walked over and knocked on the door, anxious to see this new boy or girl who was stealing my friend. Then I heard a man's voice yell, "Just a minute!"

He was at the door, opening it just a crack, then more when he saw me. It was the guy I always saw there. "Come in!" he said, too much excitement in his voice. "We were just watching a movie."

Vanessa stood in the hall between the living room and the back bedroom, alternating between looking down and then at me, again and again. He was also looking back and forth at us, I guess trying to tell what we were saying to each other without words. *Top Gun* was on, Goose and Maverick turning and looping through the air. The movie just kept playing, none of us looking at the TV. I had interrupted something.

"Do you want juice?" he asked, moving to the kitchen to get it before waiting for an answer. "Vanessa, sit and watch the movie," he said, and then to me, "Have you seen *Top Gun*? I have a lot of movies to watch." He pointed to the room that in our house was the junk room left to the rats. Here, the room was floor-to-ceiling shelves of VHS tapes, the names of films taped off the TV scrawled on the side. Every eighties film you can imagine, he had.

He was suddenly behind me. "Come sit," he said. "Watch the movie." Vanessa was on the couch, still not talking. I sat next to her, and he seemed flustered, as if he wanted to sit between us. Vanessa and I watched the movie, but he kept looking at us. On-screen, Goose ejected during a firefight, hit the cockpit glass, and fell dead into the ocean. Maverick was cradling him in the water.

"Vanessa," he said, "I have to tell you something."

She ignored him, so I answered. "What?"

"Come on, Vanessa," he said. "Come in the back and talk to me."

I made a decision. Whatever was back there, I needed to know about. "No," I said. "I wanna go in the back and talk to you."

He got up quickly and walked down the hall. "It's a secret," he said. When I entered, he closed the door behind me.

I was wearing the hot pink cotton bicycle shorts that were so big in the eighties and a huge shirt my mom got at Kmart. It was white and had three girls on it holding surfboards with raised puffy paint designs. I looked down at my clear jelly sandals, the ones I loved so much even though they made everyone's feet smell so bad. He took off my clothes, and the feeling I most remember is shock at what was happening.

I was nine. I was a child, and then I wasn't.

It was the start of two years of this man sexually assaulting me. He was raping Vanessa, so I put myself between them, continually offering myself up so he would leave her alone. She was fragile and younger, I thought in my kid logic, and I was not. I would bike to her home, and when I realized she was inside his house, I would bang on the door until he let me in. There would be the pretense of watching a movie, which would lead to him making a move on Vanessa and me demanding that he "talk" to me instead. Everything would be finished by four thirty, when his wife would come home from work.

In summer, the assault was near daily. Vanessa's mom watched a boy my age, Randy, who tried to get in to watch movies. "He's a boy," the man told us, "so he can't come in." You're asking why Vanessa went over there so much. I know, I did, too. I can't guess what hold he had on her. I don't blame her, because she was a child doing what an adult told her she was supposed to do. I blame the adults in our lives. How did her mom let her be there every day for hours, feet from her house, and not know? Vanessa's mom was deeply religious and very traditional, way more protective of her daughter than my disappearing-act mom. Why was this such a blind spot?

A year into the abuse, when I was ten, I slept over at Vanessa's house. We were up playing past lights-out, just these two normal kids feeling naughty for staying up. When I started to get tired, I figured I should go pee. The hallway was dark, but there was light in the living room. Her parents had people over, a man and a woman. As I crept to the bathroom, I noticed they were using the hushed whispers that grown-ups talk in when they're trying not to be overheard. The voice that automatically lets you know they're talking about something that you're not supposed to hear. Which of course just makes you want to hear it. I crept just a little farther down.

"I just don't see why you let her play with Vanessa," said the male friend.

"I don't know," her dad said. "We try to do what's right and not judge, but yeah, she's white trash."

"The poor thing's never gonna amount to nothing," Vanessa's mother said. "Not with that mama. Vanessa's room will smell like cigarettes tomorrow. Watch."

"She smokes?" asked the female friend.

"Naw, it's that mom," said Vanessa's mother.

"She will soon enough," said Vanessa's dad, "and probably try to get Vanessa into it."

They moved on to the weather, having decimated me. My face was burning hot, and I walked into the bathroom and quietly closed the door before I started sobbing. I looked in the mirror and for the first time I saw what they saw. The dirty clothes, the hair my mother never touched. I pulled up my T-shirt, first to wipe my eyes, then to try to huff in the smell of smoke that maybe I had grown used to. All this time, these people thought I was trash. My mother's neglect, being sexually abused next door, just twenty feet away from where they were sitting discussing me—it was all to be expected for someone who wouldn't amount to anything.

And then I got angry. I washed my face, slapping cold water on it to stop my crying. I leaned in toward the mirror, and I said two little words that have made all the difference.

"Fuck them," I whispered. I was going to prove them wrong. It was the start of a coping mechanism that has gotten me through every traumatic event in my life: I keep moving. I'm not the kind of person to stay in one place. If I'm not going forward, I know I will go backward. So I just keep going.

It's part of why I never sought help from an adult to stop the abuse. I thought that would just affirm what people thought about me. I suppose that's what a serial abuser counts on—the notion that kids blame themselves. If you didn't tell the first time, it's harder to tell the second time. Vanessa's parents would probably think I liked it. Besides, in my world, adults were not people who helped you. I was on my own protecting Vanessa, and taking her place was the only way I knew how. And when adults did get involved, they let us down. I am sure there were other girls he raped, because when I was eleven years old, near the end of the summer of 1990, he got into trouble when he made some kind of move on the visiting family member of another neighbor girl. She told her parents, who called the cops.

The police showed up at my house, two men at the door. My mom happened to be home, and she opened the door just a crack to talk to them. I stood in the living room as they talked quietly. I heard my name, and she told them, "Hold on," and closed the door.

She said the man's name. "They wanna know if he's ever done anything inappropriate," she said. "If there's something you need to tell me, you tell me privately. Because if I let them in they'll take you away and I'll never see you again."

My mom looked around the room quickly—there was a glimmer of shame I'd never seen from her about the state of the house. The bugs and the rats, the filth surrounding us. She was right—anyone in their right mind would take a child out of that house.

"No," I said. I am a terrible liar, and my mother knew it. She just didn't want to let the police see how we were living. She opened the door again, still just an inch.

"She said he's never done anything to her," my mom said flatly. "Okay? Bye." My mom closed the door on them and any discussion about what had really been happening to me. She lit a cigarette and never brought it up again.

As far as I know, he never did any jail time, but Vanessa stopped going over there. I don't know if he was spooked or her parents told her to stop going. Vanessa and I drifted apart as friends when I started seventh grade at Istrouma Middle Magnet School around that time. When I saw her, she acted like I was just someone she knew vaguely. I accepted that, because I was already doing my own work of burying the abuse and moving on as if it had never happened. I started "dating" a boy at school, meaning we held hands and wrote each other notes. Michael lived down the block from me and had brown hair and the cutest nose. We dated for a few months and he was so great—until he dumped me on Valentine's Day. He did it just as all the other girls were getting their valentines, and I have always suspected that he broke up with me to avoid the embarrassment of telling me he didn't get me a card.

Not long after, we were getting off the bus from the school, him behind me, and he grabbed my ass. He had done things like that before, but now we weren't dating. I reacted with an insane fury, with all my pent-up anger focused on him. I pushed him, and when he pushed me back, I lunged at him, jumping him and throwing him to the ground. While other kids watched, we rolled around someone's front yard, with me punctuating my slaps and blows with "That. Is. Not. Okay."

He got away from me, and we called it a draw. "You do not get to do that," I yelled.

"Okay," he said, dusting himself off. "Okay."

Someone told on us, and since we were just coming off the bus we got suspended for a day. They called our parents in and my mom actually showed up. His mom, Terry, a bus driver, came in, and seemed relieved that Michael and I had already made up. But my mom made a scene, making the most of the attention on her. As Michael and I sat in little plastic chairs outside Principal Patim's, we could hear my mother rant inside. When Mr. Patim refused to lift the suspension, my mother stood on his desk and yelled, "You just taught my daughter that it's okay to be sexually assaulted."

Michael and I exchanged a wide-eyed look. For him, it was insane to see and hear a parent acting that crazy, saying those words. But as I waited for my mom's performance to end, I played the words over in my head, "sexually assaulted." That is what had happened to me for two years, and she knew. If anyone had tried to teach me that I needed to be "okay" with being raped, it was her. As an accomplice in silencing me, maybe this was the alibi she was telling herself: her daughter's first brush with assault was a boy grabbing her butt, not the continual rape she chose to believe never happened because it would have exposed her negligence.

The following year, Vanessa started at my middle school and was having crippling anxiety. There was an incident, I don't know what, but it was enough of one that she had to see a guidance counselor. She told him what she had been through. I guess she said my name, because he called me in.

"Is what Vanessa is saying happened to her true?" he said, looking across the desk at me.

"Yes," I said.

"Were you there?"

"Yes," I said, and finally I was able to say it. "He did it to me, too."

"Why are you saying that?"

"Saying what?" I asked. "He—"

"Vanessa has real problems," he said. "He didn't touch you."

"He did, I swear."

"Then why are *you* fine?"

"I don't know," I said. Was I?

"Because you're making it up," he said. "I don't know why you would lie about this. Are you jealous of the attention she's getting? Is that it?"

"No," I said.

"Then why would you lie?"

I didn't answer. I looked at my hands until he told me to leave. I'd finally outright asked for help from an adult, and I was called a liar. Vanessa stopped talking to me altogether, pretending I didn't exist if we walked by each other in the hall. She seemed to hold her breath until I was gone, like kids do when they pass a cemetery. I respected that and didn't push her. Maybe I reminded her of the room, or maybe she felt responsible for what that man had done to me.

Vanessa and I still have mutual friends, so I know she has created a nice life doing the profession she dreamed about doing as a kid. I hesitated to even share this here because I know how quickly my truth will be used against me by people who want to prove that women involved in the adult entertainment business are all "damaged." In a recent survey of two thousand people, 81 percent of the women alleged they had experienced sexual harassment or assault. Did they all become porn stars? By that logic, if you polled a hundred female surgeons—or politicians—would none of the women say that they got through growing up female scot-free? Vanessa and I endured assaults from the same man. Why isn't she doing porn?

After the guidance counselor, I never told a single person about the sexual abuse until this past June. I had been so successful blocking out what happened to me that it only came up when I recently went back to my old horseshoe neighborhood for a profile of my life. To show them my childhood home, we had to drive by the house where I was continually assaulted. Seeing it brought back a flood of feelings, and I broke down. I am still receiving flashes of memory, moments too graphic and sickening for me to share. Mainly it just hurts to remember being that vulnerable.

Being a rape survivor does not define me at all. If anything, what was ingrained into me was the expectation that I would not be believed if I ever asked for help. It's why I keep highlighting this whole passage, my finger hovering over the Delete key. What stops me is seeing a bracelet on my right hand, a blue rubber one that I give out to people at events. In white type there is a quote from me: "Standing up to bullies is kind of my thing."

I may not always want to, and I may fear what will happen when I do, but I have to tell the truth. This is mine.

My mom kept stumbling into dead-end relationships with guys, and Wade would still come around to sit in the front room. That only ended when she started dating Sidney Kelley. He was really nice and had a good job. What was the draw for my mom? you might wonder. Well, he was also a raging alcoholic. He had four kids of his own already. A boy, Trey, who was a year younger than me, and a set of Satan twins, two girls who were four years younger than me. They lived with their mom, Carla. He also had a bonus baby, Hope, who lived with her mom. She was two years old and the reason he was no longer with Carla.

I was told to call him Mr. Kelley, and that continued even after my mom married him when I was eleven and he became my stepdad. He moved in with us, and my mom found a new villain in Carla. "Carla's such a bitch and she doesn't want the kids over" was a constant refrain. Well, I wouldn't want my kids in that filthy house, either. Team Carla here.

Mr. Kelley drank all the time and would be falling-down drunk around the neighbors. Even in our increasingly trashy neighborhood, it was like *Whoa*. One time at home he fell into the picture window. He hit it with his head and it shattered but didn't break. They taped it up and it stayed shattered all through middle school and high school. It stayed that way for ten years.

In seventh grade, I met a girl name Myranda who was a year younger than me. I was walking by her when she mentioned to her friend that she wasn't taking the bus because her mom was picking her up for a riding lesson.

"Hi," I said, immediately latching on to her. I may as well have said, "Hi, new best friend. You're going to be my friend whether you like it or not." She was woefully ignorant about the riding lessons, so I realized I needed to speak to a manager. Her mom.

"Tell me about these riding lessons," I said. "Where do you go?" This was pre-internet, and my mom knew nothing about horses. I needed to make this happen. I had her call my mom to tell her about it, and I started taking lessons with a trainer named Miss Cathy at four thirty in the afternoon every Wednesday.

Myranda's mom would pick us up from school and drive us out to the barn, and she would often take me home, too.

For months, my entire week revolved around Wednesdays.

A week before Christmas 1991, my stepdad Mr. Kelley told me he was going to pick me up that night when my lesson was over. He was getting his Christmas bonus and he was going to take me shopping so I could buy presents for people and myself.

I sat in the barn waiting. Myranda's mom came and lingered, twice asking if maybe she could just take me home. "No, thank you," I said. My riding instructor, Miss Cathy, busied herself tending to a pathetic horse that had been returned that day. Her name was Perfect Jade, and she was rail thin and had clearly been abused since leaving the barn. She was covered in fungus and was so mangy, I couldn't tell what color she was. She was mean from all her mistreatment, and Miss Cathy told me to stay clear.

When Mr. Kelley finally showed up, he was shit-faced.

"I'm not getting in the car," I said. Miss Cathy came over and immediately took stock of the situation.

"She can stay here until Sheila gets off work," she said.

"Come on," he said.

"She can stay here," Cathy said, in the same tone she used to show a horse who was in charge.

"Well, she's been wanting a horse for Christmas," he slurred. "So how much does a horse cost?"

"Well, Chiffon's eight grand," said Cathy.

"For a fucking horse?" he spit. I now own a fifty-thousand-dollar horse, but that would have been a lot then for Chiffon. Cathy made so much money off that horse, using it for therapy and riding. I know now if you have a horse you don't want to sell, you put a price on it no one wants to spend.

Mr. Kelley tried one more time to get me to go with him, and then finally gave up. "Well, here's the money for your presents," he said, handing me five hundred dollars cash. He got in the car and raced off.

Miss Cathy went to the office to call my mom at work. "It's a shame he didn't ask about this one," she said, gesturing to poor Perfect Jade. "I'd sell you that one for five hundred."

"Okay," I said as fast as I could reach for the money in my pocket. "Done."

And so Perfect Jade was mine. I told my mom later that Mr. Kelley bought her for me. She confronted him about it the next day, but he'd been so drunk he didn't remember what happened. No one was going to take my horse away from me.

When Miss Cathy gave me Perfect Jade's papers, I knew it was meant to be. We had the same St. Patrick's Day birthday, though she was two years older. She was an ex-racehorse, and because she was a Thoroughbred, her papers listed her bloodlines. Her grandfather was Bold Ruler, an American Thoroughbred Hall of Fame racehorse who was named 1957 Horse of the Year. His broodmare grandmother, Primonetta, was one of the top fillies in American racing in 1961, and when she died of a heart attack just shy of thirty-five years old in 1993, she was the third-longest-lived filly known to horse racing. Jade's bloodlines were so good, I am sure they probably tried to breed her at some point and it just didn't take.

But looking at her when I met her, you would never know she came from glory. She had this pencil-thin neck with a mane that was so long. She had patches of hair missing from fungus, and what hair she did have was sun-bleached.

Now I had a horse, but I didn't own anything for a horse. I didn't have a saddle or bridle, but I couldn't put a saddle on her anyway because she was so skinny. With no padding, it would have just rubbed blisters on her. I had to fatten her up first, but I didn't mind because I just wanted to be near horses, period. I became obsessed with her, leading her up and down the road like a dog to get her strength up.

I loved her, but man she was mean. She would chase me out, snapping her teeth at me. If I went to pick up her back feet, she'd poop on me. I know that fucking bitch was doing it on purpose. Every time I'd turn my back she would bite the shit out of me and break skin.

One time I was feeding her and she bit me so hard, I had enough. I grabbed her ear and I bit her back. "You see?" I screamed through tears. "That *hurts!*"

It was a come-to-Jesus moment for us. After that, she never hurt me again.

When her hair came in that summer, it was black and sleek. Jade had grown back to being a big black mare, all filled out. She was breathtaking. I started riding her and learned everything on that horse. I was able to board her at my boyfriend Jacob Bailey's barn. The Baileys were a farming family, so they kept a barn down the street from their house, which was close to a river. I visited Jade just about every day. And Jacob. We were both thirteen and had started dating the summer between seventh and eighth grades. He was so cute—super

Christian, with an extremely conservative family. He taught me how to clean a gun and how to ride four-wheelers. Every day he would ride his four-wheeler alongside me and Jade as we galloped in the sand along the river. He could just keep up with us. He even built jumps for me as I became interested in eventing. Eventing is the equestrian triathlon, with three disciplines in one competition. There's dressage, which is considered one of the highest forms of horse training. Then cross-country, where you and your horse navigate an outdoor obstacle course. And finally, jumping, which is specifically about clearing fences.

In December, I was at the barn cleaning Jade's stall when Jacob got called home for dinner. It was freezing cold. Baton Rouge can still have mild weather during the day that time of year, but it can dip down to the thirties and forties at night.

"Your mom's coming soon, right?" he said. We were both thirteen, but we looked out for each other in that way.

"Yeah," I said. She was supposed to be there at six o'clock. Six went by, then seven. I didn't have a cell phone to call her, so I didn't know if or when she'd show up. I was too embarrassed to walk over to Jacob's house. I sat in the feed room, hugging myself for warmth.

Around eight, Jacob's mother saw the barn's lights were still on, so she sent Jacob down. She thought I'd left without turning them off. Jacob walked in and I held out my arms to hug him. He put his coat on me, and I kissed him. We started making out, and, as they say, one thing led to another. It was my choice, and I felt completely safe with him. We had sex on top of a deep freeze they used as a feed bin. It was the first time making love for both of us, and I was blessed and cursed that I had an orgasm. It sounds good, but do you know how hard it was to find a boy to do that for the next fifteen years?

After that night, we fucked like bunnies. We would go up in the hayloft to have sex. It was always furtive and half-dressed. I don't think I ever even saw his penis. His family was so religious that this was all wrapped up in sin.

This went on into the summer before ninth grade, when we were found out. No one ever walked in on us, as far as I know, but his parents sat him down. They told him he could never see me again, and he followed their orders. They made me move Jade out of their barn and let me know that I was a piece of white-trash shit.

This piece of shit had the straight As to get into a magnet school, so come ninth grade, I didn't see him again anyway. Scotlandville Magnet High School, an engineering school with a focus on science and math, was about five miles from my house, but they would bus you out. It was better than going to my neighborhood school, where I probably would have been killed. I wanted Baton Rouge High because they were known for their arts programs in dance and writing, but they were full and on the wrong side of town.

Writing was all I wanted to do besides ride Jade. English was my favorite subject, and I took creative writing classes. Later I would get into all the AP English classes and become editor of my high school newspaper. With my photographic memory and an eye for detail, storytelling came naturally to me. I would always finish my work early in class, and to pass time while everyone else finished tests, I would write funny short stories about me and my friends. They were basically scripts, embellished versions of what was going on in our lives. Exactly what I do now when I write scripts for films. Just like my high school friends, my friends know that they need to be careful around me. They'll tell me something funny that happened to them, and they'll recognize that funny look on my face as I press Record in my mind.

"Oh, shit," they'll say. "I'm a script now, aren't I?"

"You totally are," I answer.

Back in high school, the star of most of my friend stories was my best friend, Elizabeth. We sat alphabetically in class, and her last name fell right after Gregory, so she was always right behind me from the first day of ninth grade. She had come from a small private school and knew absolutely no one at school, whereas I had moved with a crew. I turned around to say hi the first day and she was wearing a pale pink T-shirt that showed a row of cats walking from behind, their tails in the air.

"I'm sorry, is that a line of cat buttholes on your shirt?" I asked.

Elizabeth looked down, pulling her shirt out to get a better look. "I guess so," she said.

"Okay, we're going to be friends," I said. "Because you really need one."

Boy crazy and Catholic, she was the perfect wingwoman. She worked at McDonald's all through high school, and I could always count on her to feed me free food when I was hungry, which was often. To this day, when Elizabeth and I are in the same room we are those two girls again, talking over each other about some boy and laughing. Thank God for those cat butts.

When I had to move Jade so abruptly from Jacob's barn, I boarded her at Farr Park Equestrian Center. It became my real home. I got special permission from my high school to take a bus every day down to the LSU campus area, so I could then walk two miles south to go see her. I knew I'd lose Jade if I couldn't afford to board her, so I started working at Farr Park, whether it was teaching kids at their summer horse camp or doing secretarial work in the office. I did anything to keep Jade with me.

I began taking lessons with a trainer, Nancy Burba, and I worked off the payment by exercising her horses. On the weekends, we started doing horse shows. At one point, somebody offered me fifteen thousand dollars for Jade. That kind of money would have been life changing, but I didn't think about it for even a second. "She's not for sale," I said. Besides, Jade wouldn't let anyone else ride her, and she wouldn't perform for anyone else, either.

Never once did I fall off of that horse. Not one single time, which is a miracle, because it's just a fact that you come off your horses. Whether they dump you or they spook, you come off. It's not if you get hurt, it's when. And how bad.

She protected me, too. We were out galloping one day, riding through a neighborhood the city was starting to develop. It had been a while since I'd ridden back there, so I didn't know that they had dug huge drainage canals, about twenty feet across. The grass had gotten tall, so we were going full speed and I didn't see the new canal until two strides out. I felt Jade see it and I could tell she was thinking, *Fuck it, I won't be able to stop.* She leapt into the air, clearing the twenty-foot jump.

I was so scared that when I got to the other side, I got down from Jade. "Oh, my God," I said, walking in a circle, kicking out my legs, which one second ago I was sure would be broken. "Oh, my God." Jade nuzzled me and I looked her in the eye.

"Good job," I said.

People who knew Jade's history told me I saved that horse, but she saved me. Since I hated being home, if I hadn't had the barn to go I would have just hung around my little crack neighborhood, smoking and drinking with the other kids my age. I was too busy going to horse shows on the weekends to spend time at the mall flirting with boys. I would see yet another girl who lived around me suddenly pregnant and say to myself silently, *Can't ride a horse if you're pregnant.*

That meant that any guy who wanted to be around me had to make room for Jade. In my freshman year, I started dating Kris, a brown-haired tenth grader who was two years older than me. They'd held him back a year when his family moved over from Poland as a small child, but he was really smart, and his parents were biochemists at LSU studying carcinogens. He had a car and would drive me to the barn and all my horse events. Kris bought my first dressage saddle, so I could compete, and he would take pictures for me at all my shows. He was not going to get on a horse, but he bought a mountain bike so he could ride along with me and Jade. He taught me how to drive, and I'm actually a great driver because of him.

And he taught me how to say what I liked in bed. "Do you like when I touch you like this?" he would ask me, genuinely wanting me to enjoy our time together. Whereas Jacob was so conservative, Kris would just walk around naked in his room, comfortable with his body. We didn't do anything freaky, but we had a lot of sex, and more importantly, we could talk about it without shame.

When I was sixteen, Kris wrote a letter to my mom telling her to put me on birth control. I had been too afraid to ask her.

She was furious, but I heard her talking to her friends about it, saying she thought it was cool that he was honest and concerned about me. Two days later she thanked him and she put me on birth control. I have Kris to thank for my being able to enjoy sex without constantly worrying about getting pregnant and stuck in Baton Rouge.

Yes, Kris was the best boyfriend, until he cheated on me. But I don't blame him. We were high school kids and the girl, Camille, was really fucking hot. She had an Angelina Jolie look.

I was with my best friend, Elizabeth, when I saw them. We were in her car, driving to Coffee Call, a coffee shop on College Drive in Baton Rouge. It had been Kris's and my place. And there he was, walking in holding hands with Camille.

I sat there, my mouth open, when the radio DJ came on to present a song they'd just gotten in. Alanis Morissette's "You Oughta Know." As Alanis sang, Elizabeth got more and more wide-eyed as I just stared at the café.

"That's a really good song," I said when it was over.

"Yeah," she said, still looking at me like I was a time bomb.

"So, I'm just gonna go in there and kill him," I said.

"Cool," she said.

I did confront Kris. I didn't kill him, nor did I scream-sing my new favorite song at him. He admitted it, always honest, and that was that. But whenever I hear that song, my eyes narrow and I am right back at the Coffee Call.

I did a bank shot to sink the nine ball and glanced up at my dad. For the first time, he looked proud of me. I'd waited fifteen years for that.

We were in a bar near his house on Thorn Tree Court in Miamiville, just outside Cincinnati. Susan had been making him spend more one-on-one time with me since middle school. He tried. We would run to Subway for an hour, but he just couldn't relate to me. Now I was fifteen years old and mature enough for my age that we could finally relate.

They knew him by name when we walked in but seemed surprised that he had a daughter. It was a little bar with several pool tables, and my dad's a very good player. He started to teach me how to play, at first probably just to pass the time. But once he saw I was pretty good, he seemed more interested. He gave me money for the jukebox, and I went over but I didn't know how to make the selection. I'd never seen one before.

"Oh, it's easy," he said, coming over to show me. I looked up at him and smiled. This was what I wanted as a kid. Him showing me how to do things. "What song do you want?" he asked.

"Uh," I said, drawing it out as I flipped through the records until I saw Def Leppard. "How about 'Let's Get Rocked'?"

He nodded and smiled. "Good choice," he said. We went back to pool, and he surprised me by knowing the lyrics. We were singing and laughing, and I think he was surprised that he was actually having fun.

The next day he took me out on his boat to go waterskiing. He brought a friend with him, because you need a spotter and a driver. I picked it up pretty quickly, mainly because I was determined to impress him. I got up on the third try and as I held on, I could just see him thinking, *Oh, maybe she is mine.*

Other times we went out on the water, just me and him. He'd drink his Coors Light, and we got to a point where the awkwardness was almost gone. It was the same the following summer, when I was sixteen. When we were in his element—at a pool table or on the boat—he could just be quiet with me. I was just happy to be there.

It was around this time that Susan became the first I told about hating the name Stephanie. There are lots of stories about why I call myself Stormy, but the truth is that while Stephanie is a lovely name, it never suited me. First off, my mother gave it to me, and I didn't want anything from her. And I read a lot of books about Native Americans because of my dad's Cherokee heritage. In those stories, names reflected both character and destiny. I couldn't rule the world with a name like Stephanie. But Stormy . . . that made more sense.

But then my dad and Susan split up, and with her went the person making him hang out with me. I only saw him one more time. At the end of junior year, I was sitting in class when a voice came over the loudspeaker: "Please send Stephanie down to the office. Her dad is here to pick her up."

My best friend, Elizabeth, was in that class, and as I picked up my books she stage-whispered, *"Who?"*

I figured it had to be my stepdad, but he had never come to check me out of school. Mr. Kelley would never call himself my father, so the office lady must have seen a big guy and assumed. I walked quickly, worried something was wrong with my mom or my horse.

And there he was. My father, standing completely out of context in my school. I didn't know he even knew where I went to school.

"Is everything okay?" I asked.

"Yeah," he said. "I just wanted to see you."

"Does Mom know you're here?"

"Yeah, I just let her know," he said, the slightest grimace crossing his face. I could guess how the call went. I was surprised the school even let him take me, because he wasn't on any kind of form they had. We walked outside, and I saw he had his truck hooked up to his boat, full of stuff. It was just like all the moves we did when I was a kid.

"Me and Susan split up," he said.

"I kinda heard," I said.

"Yeah, we sold the house," he said. "I'm on my way to California."

"Oh."

"I just thought I'd take you shopping," he said, getting out his keys.

"For what?" I asked.

"How do you feel about getting a car today?"

Pretty good, actually. We hit a used-car lot and he told me I could have eight grand to spend on any car I wanted. That feels like twenty thousand these days. He told me to pick out whatever I wanted. He paid cash for a Toyota Celica that seemed pretty brand-new to me. It was dark teal, but the coolest thing about it was it had the flip-up headlights. He paid for a year of insurance on it and took me to dinner. At the restaurant, I mostly talked about how I couldn't believe I had a new car. When it was over, he got in his car and left.

I never saw him again.

I still can't figure out why he just handed me a car free and clear. It was nowhere near my birthday or graduation. Maybe it was just a final gift, so he could leave me again with a clear conscience. Eight grand to just be done with me.

This will shock you, but things weren't working out between my mom and Mr. Kelley. I know, right? We were pulling for those two kids, weren't we? Their arguments were getting increasingly frequent, and when they went at it while I was home, I just went to my room and put on my headphones. If they screamed louder, I just turned the volume up. I never got in the middle of it, and Mr. Kelley never would have hurt me.

One of the final straws was when he got out a shotgun in the house. I was on my bed, and my mom's bedroom shared a wall with mine. He shot a hole through it and the buckshot tore through my closet, ruining all my clothes. If I had been standing up, I would have been shot.

After the initial "what the fuck?" shock, I said to myself: *It might be time to get out of here.* There was one more huge fight, where they were both breaking things. We already didn't have anything, so I called Michael, the boy who'd broken up with me on Valentine's Day in the seventh grade. He lived around the corner and his dad was a police officer. I tried to get them to come over and help me, but they wouldn't. The neighborhood had disintegrated to such a point that this wasn't worth getting involved in.

Finally, Mr. Kelley left. I hear he's sober now, and I hope he's doing great. I don't blame him for leaving my mother. It was time for me to get out of Dodge, too.

The Christmas Tree Incident has become famous among my friends, because they had to witness it. The Christmas tree was still up in our front room, though it was January. On a Friday, my friend Anna was over to watch *Late Night with Conan O'Brien* with our respective boyfriends. Hers was a nice guy. And mine was Andy, who was not. At twenty years old, Andy was three years older than me and already out of school. He had long dark hair shaved on one side, ice-blue eyes, a really big penis, and a dark soul. Never toward me, but he had demons. He was super into guns and tried to be a marine to make his family proud, but he couldn't hack it. He came home and their disappointment weighed heavy on him.

My mom was in her bedroom, and the house was quiet except for Conan. Suddenly we heard this bloodcurdling scream. It scared the shit out of us, but before we could react there was a rush of feet stomping. It was my mother running, still screaming, down the hall in her forest-green silk nightgown. She passed in front of us, jumped up on a chair—and proceeded to rip off her nightgown like the Hulk.

No underwear. None. She stood naked for one second, lost her balance, and fell back into the Christmas tree.

I moved out the next morning.

Andy and I got an apartment together for $335 a month on LSU's campus. Andy had money from his job delivering pizza, and he had three thousand dollars in the bank from some relative dying. I kept going to high school like normal and kept up with my routine of visiting my horse, Jade, every day.

We had no furniture, unless you count a mattress on the floor and some plastic shelves for Andy's CDs. He loved music, though he didn't play, and had an encyclopedic knowledge of metal and hard rock. He turned me on to all the music I still listen to today: Metallica, Mötley Crüe, Ratt, Skid Row, and Poison. We would go to all-ages shows in fields to watch local bands like Acid Bath, who were my favorite. They had a song called "Bleed Me an Ocean," a line of which I still want to get tattooed on my body: "Just like a raindrop, I was born, baby, to fall." Around when I moved in with Andy that January of my senior year, Acid Bath came to an end when the bass player, Audie Pitre, and his parents were killed, hit head-on by a drunk driver over on Highway 24.

At one of those rock concerts in a field, our first weekend living together, most of the people there were around Andy's age. We were all hanging out when someone pulled up in a brand-new purple Camaro. This pretty girl got out and she was a magnet for people. Everyone wanted to know how a nineteen-year-old had a Camaro, which was like a Ferrari in 1997 Baton Rouge.

"Look at my new car," she said, as if everyone wasn't.

"Did you get this for graduation?" I asked.

She laughed. "No, I graduated two years ago," she said. "I bought this."

"You did?" I said. "What do you *do*?"

"I'm a dancer," she said.

I was studying ballet in high school and I was on the dance team, so I was thinking *Nutcracker*. "Oh, what kind of dancing do you do?"

She looked around at the people gathered, with an expression that said, *What's with this fucking chick?* "Uh, I work at Cinnamon's," she said.

Cinnamon's was a strip club, and the only reason I knew about it was because they had TV commercials. "Oh," I said. "Oh. *Ohhhhhh*."

And before I could say anything else stupid, she said, "Yeah, if you guys are ever driving by, you should stop in and I'll buy you all a drink."

At the time there was a brief window when if you were eighteen you could drink in bars, thanks to the Louisiana Supreme Court finding that a drinking age of twenty-one amounted to age discrimination. But I was not even eighteen yet—I was a seventeen-year-old high schooler. So I didn't think I'd be taking her up on the offer anytime soon.

I was wrong. Two weeks later, Andy and I were driving out by Prairieville on a Tuesday night. We had two of his friends in the back, and we drove by Cinnamon's. "Oh, my God, that's where that girl works," I said. "Amy the Camaro girl."

"You know somebody who works there?" one of the guys in the back said in this voice of excited disbelief.

"Yeah, she said we should stop in."

Andy did a movie-worthy U-turn and we drove into the gravel parking lot.

Now, there are gentlemen's clubs, then there are strip clubs, and then there are titty bars. Cinnamon's was a titty bar. Basically, a trailer. It wasn't even nice enough to be in Baton Rouge—it was across the bridge in Prairieville.

I panicked when I saw there was a bouncer checking IDs. The three guys were all over eighteen, so they got in just fine. When it was my turn, I reached into my purse, stalling by fumbling for my wallet. "Oh, yeah, lemme . . . ," I said. I had it in my hand, and a little voice in my head said to do something.

"Hey, is *Amy* working tonight?" I said her name like it was a magical spell. And it worked.

"Yeah," he said, softening. "You're friends with Amy?"

"She invited us."

"Why didn't you say something? Come on in!"

He never checked my ID. It was in my hand and he never reached for it. I crossed the threshold of Cinnamon's and saw that our arrival had more than doubled the number of customers there. Tuesday nights were slow, I guessed. There was a guy playing video poker, and the ceiling was so low, you could reach your hand up to touch it.

Amy came out like we were old pals and bought us drinks. The guys couldn't believe their luck. Amy called over to the dancers, "Come meet my friends!"

The girls started coming over, bored and looking for something new to talk about. A range of ages from twenties to thirties, they were all talking to me at once.

"You're so pretty. You should do a guest set."

"Have you ever danced before?"

"Where do you dance?"

"I'm still in school," I said.

Only later did I realize everyone thought I meant LSU.

"We're just going to borrow her," Amy said to Andy.

They spirited me into the dressing room, a long rectangle with a table and chairs. It was very smoky and dirty, with two steps that went up the back to the DJ booth, which you walked through to get up to a stage that was the size of a queen-size bed. The girls began to play dress-up with me. I was Cinderella, with the bluebirds and mice making my dress and fairy godmothers making me feel special.

They muttered and cooed over their project. "Try this on," a blonde said, handing me a bustier. Another girl said they were going to just do a little something with my eyebrows, and they all nodded. One girl got to plucking, and it hurt so much, but

I'm thankful for it now. You should have seen those brows. I'd never groomed them, because my mother didn't teach me any of that stuff. They did my makeup and did what they could with my brown hair, which I'd always just worn long and flat.

"What's your name?" Amy asked me.

"Stormy," I said, looking at my transformation in the mirror. I smiled. *Stormy.*

My fairy godmothers talked me into doing a guest set. "It's two songs," said Amy. "The first is up-tempo and dressed, the second is slower and more sensual as you go topless."

I told the DJ that I would start with "Looks That Kill" by Mötley Crüe and then do "Love You to Death" by Type O Negative. He turned to a virtual wall of CDs behind him, at least four hundred, and immediately grabbed what he needed.

"I'm Dalton," he said. "I'll announce you, so what's your name?"

"Stormy."

"You want that to be your stage name?"

"Well, my real name is Stephanie, but—"

"Stephanie Stormy," he said. "Got it."

"Wait . . ."

It was too late. The music started and "Stephanie Stormy" took the stage. I was already a dancer, so I was comfortable doing that and knew how to do little movements that would look pretty. The girls were so supportive and were cheering me on and tipping me through my first song. A few more guys had come in and had a look of "We're gonna see new titties!" The bartender came from behind the bar and tipped me, and so did the bouncer. Andy looked very proud.

The second song started and I thought, *Here we go.* I took my top off and no one laughed. *Hunh*. Cinnamon, the owner, came out of the office to watch. She was so beautiful, like a young Madeleine Stowe, with long, long dark hair. When the song was over I did a quick bow and discreetly tried to pick up all the dollar bills. I made eighty-five dollars, more money in those two songs than I made answering phones all week at the barn.

The girls ran backstage to hug me, and Cinnamon came in, too.

"Do you want a job?" she asked.

"I have school, so I can't work during the week," I said.

"Well, can you do Friday and Saturday nights?"

Eighty-five dollars in nine minutes. "Yeah," I said.

TWO

The first rule of Cinnamon's—the only rule, really—was that you could not be topless on the floor. As the Louisiana State Legislature dictated, "Entertainers whose breasts or buttocks are exposed to view shall perform only upon a stage at least eighteen inches above the immediate floor. . . ." No woman's feet shall touch earth if she is showing her boobs for dollars. Amen.

At many clubs, if a customer requests a private dance, you could raise your hand straight high in the air and a bouncer would bring over a little box for you to stand on. But Cinnamon's was so small that they didn't even have room for boxes. If you wanted to give somebody a dance, you took them in the back room where they had a mini stage set up. There was a squiggly curve we could stand on next to each other, and the guys sat on rolling chairs.

My first Friday night at Cinnamon's I heard this rule about ten times in the first ten minutes I was there. "It's the easiest way for cops to bust up the place," said Cinnamon.

"I get it," I said. "The floor is lava."

"Lava," she said. "If you do a dance, you absolutely have to put your dress back on before you get down."

I didn't have good dancing clothes, so I had bought a dress cheap from the club. It was red velvet, and I paired it with white heels from home. It didn't take long before a guy asked for a dance. He was okay looking, a skinny guy with brown hair. I led him to the back room and tried to look like I knew what I was doing.

I took the spot right next to Tracy, who was this total biker chick. She was the wife of one of the Banditos, a local motorcycle club. She'd been a stripper all her life, pretty but ridden hard and put away wet. Beef jerky in a slingshot G-string that went up top on her shoulders, always accessorized with thighhigh leather biker boots.

We were about three feet apart, and she had just started a dance for this shifty-looking bald guy. I started dancing for my guy, which was awkward enough my first time, but I was also watching her, sneaking looks to get a sense of what I should be doing.

I took off my dress, and the guy seemed so into it. Good start, but now what? *What do I do with the dress?* I didn't want to throw it on the floor, so I wrapped it around my guy's shoulders and played with it like a sexy scarf.

Right next to me, Tracy turned her back on the guy and bent over so he could see her ass. *Noted,* I thought. *I'll do that near the end.* I had just returned my focus to my guy when all hell broke loose right next to me.

As Tracy bent over, her tampon string was sticking out of her G-string. Now, I have seen this happen twice my entire stripping career. But it was so much worse than that. The guy had tried to light the string with a cigarette lighter. Tracy saw it between her legs, and in one swift move of superhuman strength, she pulled her boot right off by the heel and repeatedly swung it down on her guy to beat the shit out of him.

"What the fuck?" I screamed, trying not to get hit.

My guy ran past me out of the club, a horny Wile E. Coyote escaping with my dress still on his shoulders. I had no dress, only a G-string, and I was three feet away from Tracy pummeling the fuck out of this guy. *And the ground was lava.*

Do you think Cinnamon's had security cameras? No, they had a video baby monitor that the bartender would periodically check. It took the bartender, who was also the bouncer that night, a couple of minutes before he came in to pull Tracy off the guy.

"I'm sorry, I thought she was a firecracker!" the guy yelled as he was thrown out the door onto the gravel.

"Tracy, you can't do that," said the bartender.

"He lit my vagina on fire!" she yelled. "Kitty had a tail and he lit it!"

Meanwhile, I was still standing on the squiggle stage, covering my breasts like this scaredy cat.

"What are you doing?" the bartender asked.

"The guy took my dress," I said, looking down at the lava floor.

"Oh, God, you can get down," he said. "It's not that serious. When there's somebody getting killed, you can leave."

"Good to know," I said. Someone let me borrow a dress. And that, folks, was my first thirty minutes as a stripper.

I grew to love Tracy and every single girl who worked there. There were less than twenty total, about six girls working a night, which is nothing. You got to pick your own music, and to this day I will hear a song and my mind goes to seeing one girl dancing to it, all of her signature moves and favorite outfits.

Tracy *only* danced to Ozzy Osbourne's "Crazy Train," so you would hear it about twenty-five freaking times a night. She was all big and bad until her man would come in the club with all his bikers.

Then there was Amy, the one who I met at the concert. I think of her when I hear Heart's "Magic Man." She was this little tiny thing with a huge ass, and she would walk, not really dance. Her big move was to bend down so her hair fell forward, then arch her body to throw it back.

I can't forget Mercedes in her white nighties, always dancing to Ratt. She was this tall, super-leggy blonde, and she barely fit on the stage. Her go-to was a vertical split, lifting her leg until her foot was flat on the ceiling. Then she'd start bumping the pole with her pussy. She wore classic nineties pumps, and she had to take one off as she raised her leg or she'd be too tall to do the trick. Mercedes had these great, natural boobs, but the main thing I remember is that she had found these baby ducks with no mom and was caring for them. She brought a little kiddie pool into the dressing room on weekends and there would be these brown ducklings wading around.

Billie was a fitness model who drove a white Chrysler 300, so I am pretty sure she had sugar daddies. She only came in to work for emergencies, usually two days before her rent was due. Then there was Venus, a lesbian who I thought was so hot. And Phoebe, tall and skinny with a pixie cut, hate-dancing to Lords of Acid's "Pussy." She'd hit her heels hard on the stage, but in the dressing room she was always crying, pleading with whoever was on the phone to let her see her kid. "You promised I could see him tomorrow" was the litany every weekend. He was about three, and she had to go to court to try to see him, but they used a solicitation charge against her. She danced with anger.

The oldest, Cheryl, was in her late forties and very pretty. She was a grandmother, which I couldn't get my head around at the time. Now I feel like I am hurtling toward that age. She was older and made no secret that she'd had a rough life, but she was unfailingly kind. Her good soul shone through and made her beautiful.

These women raised me, doing the job my mother had bowed out of. Thanks to them, I learned I was putting in tampons wrong. They taught me how to shave my bikini line so it wouldn't break out, and how to do makeup. I saw this weird little contraption on the dressing room table and blurted out, "What is that fucking thing?"

"It's an eyelash curler," said Cheryl.

"You're supposed to curl your lashes?" I asked.

"Oh, sweetie," said Mercedes.

"Raised by wolves," sighed Cheryl, fixing her lipstick.

I grew up in a strip club, and like all the dancers, I called Cinnamon "Mom." My grades never suffered, and no one from school ever knew except for my best friend, Elizabeth. My trainer, Nancy, had introduced me to her husband, Dr. Dan, at the LSU veterinary school just down the street from the barn. I started working there after school, and the highlight was caring for a foal. I applied to a veterinary school in Texas, and in the spring I was accepted with a scholarship. But I still worried about living expenses.

I was the baby at Cinnamon's, though no one knew just how young. The weekend before my March 17 birthday in 1997, they got me a cake. HAPPY 19TH BIRTHDAY! it read. But it would be my eighteenth birthday, one of the worst days of my life.

There were subtle signs, then an avalanche. Around the time I moved in with Andy, I noticed that Jade seemed a little more timid about jumps. By then, we'd had each other seven years, so we could read each other. I became much more concerned in February, when she started a rapid decline. She had consistent diarrhea and seemed increasingly listless. I led her over to Dr. Dan at the veterinary office where I worked. He had always done checkups and let me work off the payments in the office, or simply didn't charge us. He did a full workup on her and even tested her for toxins to make sure she hadn't been poisoned. He wondered if maybe she had a heart murmur, and we took a wait-and-see approach.

Then she deteriorated quickly, and by the first week of March she was wasting away. Her hair became dull and she resembled the poor, pathetic horse she had been when I first got her. I knew she had been through a lot of abuse before I had her, but she was only twenty. The average lifespan of a horse is about twenty-eight, plus or minus a few years. But she had rapidly gone from doing these huge jumps to looking like she was near death.

The last day I rode her, I knew it was the end. Spring had come and an early run of warm weather had coaxed out all the yellow butterweeds and buttercups along the trail. That day with Jade there was a sudden cold snap, so it was surreal for it to be so cold yet still have wildflowers all over. I put Jade's blanket on her to ride her—she was too thin to saddle her up, and this would keep her warm. We did a trail ride and I told her I loved her. I knew what I had to do, and afterward, I went to Dr. Dan.

"It's not fair to her," I told Dr. Dan. "She's so miserable."

"I know," he said. "I agree."

We decided to put her down, and the only time they could schedule it for was March 17, our shared birthday. I wanted to be there for it. I knew this would be bad. If you are picturing it like the gentle passing of a dog, nestled in a blanket, you're wrong. Horses don't curl up and die after they get a lethal injection. Their reaction is pretty violent, with the horse collapsing and sometimes rearing back.

All the vets came in to support us. I didn't cry much because I had already said good-bye on the trail. They let me braid her forelock so they could give it to me after, and I talked to her as I separated and twisted the hair. I told her not to be scared.

And then she was gone.

They pulled her shoes to give me, everyone tearing up. They never sent me a bill or expected anything from me for the care and kindness. Because this was a veterinary school, I knew they were going to examine the body to learn what went wrong. A couple of weeks later I was at the barn, still working just to be around horses, when a few of the vets came over to me, seeming shell-shocked.

"Jade had been operating on one valve of her heart," one told me.

"It had been dead for so long that her heart was a different color," said the other. "We don't understand how she was *walking*, much less jumping." He went on to explain that what caused the sudden deterioration was that she stopped absorbing food from scarring in her stomach after years of parasites. She was just destroyed on the inside.

Jade came into my life when I needed her, and she left when I needed her to leave. I had an apartment and plans for school. I couldn't afford her anymore, and at eighteen, I couldn't be tethered to a horse. I had to move on, and she let me. I've had so many horses since Jade, but she was the best I ever had.

I graduated from Scotlandville Magnet High School with straight As and a goal of deferring college for a year. I was "taking a year off," I told everyone. I wanted to continue working, build up savings, and then be able to focus on my studies when the time came. I taught summer camp at the equestrian center for five dollars an hour and continued dancing at Cinnamon's for a lot more. I started dyeing my hair red and noticed that I made more money as a redhead than with my natural dark hair. I made $325 one night and thought I'd won the lottery. I actually went shopping for once, which I had trained myself not to do. I was so proud of being self-sufficient that I put a bumper sticker on my Toyota Celica. It read, FOLLOW ME TO CINNAMON'S.

At the very end of August, I started having symptoms that felt like strep. My throat was on fire and I had a fever so high I was hallucinating. I didn't want to go to the doctor because I didn't have insurance and I knew it would be a fifty-dollar visit, plus whatever for the medicine. It was the weekend, and I was already out the money from missing some work at Cinnamon's. Finally, my boyfriend Andy got so worried about me that he dragged me to a clinic on Sunday, August 31.

The doctor prescribed Cefalexin. Now, there's nothing wrong

with some cephalosporins among friends, but it turned out I was allergic. I took the first dose, not knowing it was a time bomb in my body. Andy went to work, delivering pizzas late into the night, while I lay on our mattress on the floor. By then we had an old TV, but no cable. It had rabbit ears, so it would randomly catch a signal every now and again. But I had it on for white noise.

The itch started in my left arm, but gradually it spread throughout my body, going deep, as if it was in my veins. I was also having trouble breathing, still feverish and now slipping in and out of sleep.

A little after eleven at night, the TV switched from dead air to picking up NBC. I was too weak to look up, but I could hear it. Princess Diana had been badly injured in a car crash in Paris. Soon, Brian Williams was flickering in and out of my subconscious, his updates playing out in my fever dream. The itching under my skin intensified to a point that I reached for a cassette case, shook out the tape and insert card, and broke it in half. I brought the sharp edge to my arm to cut at the itch. I scratched myself up, and the pain masked the itch for just a few moments.

I was still in and out at 1 A.M. when Brian Williams returned to my little fucked-up, feverish universe to tell me Diana was dead. Andy came home at about two in the morning and found me incoherent. He'd heard the news about Diana at work, but I was telling him about it as if the whole thing was my bad fever dream. Like my mind and the world had somehow become porous.

Andy knew that he needed to take me back to the doctor, but he didn't have the money. This tells you how desperate he was: he called my mom.

"She's really sick," Andy said.

My mom said something to him, and before he could answer, she hung up on him. I asked him what she said, and he didn't say.

Andy had guns—it was Andy and it was Louisiana—so the first thing he did Monday morning was sell one for cash to take me to the doctor. They diagnosed the allergic reaction, and with the wrong medicine leaving my system and the right one doing the job, I began to feel better right away. I still have light scars on my arms from the cassette case.

"Hey," I said, sitting back at home later, able to eat the cold pizza he'd brought from work. "What did my mother say on the phone?"

"It doesn't matter," he said.

"What did she say?"

He sighed. "She said, 'She abandoned me and I fucking *hope* she dies.'"

"Wow," I said. "I abandoned *her*? I abandoned *her*?"

In March 2018, just days before my birthday, my mother and father each gave interviews to a Texas newspaper about me and President Trump. My mom told the reporter, who probably believed her, "My friends all say the same thing: 'I can't believe that is the same sweet child—you took such good care of her.'" My father professed to be worried I might come to harm for telling the truth about Trump's attempts to silence me. "You start rattling the cage of powerful people, and you don't know what might happen," he said. Right below his quote, mind you, the newspaper provided a photograph of my home and detailed the neighborhood where I live. You know, just in case anyone wanted to kill me.

I was hurt by my mom's revisionist history—at least my dad was honest in his interview about being MIA all my life—so I posted the article on the private Facebook account I keep for my friends and chosen family. Without much prompting, my childhood friends had a field day. Travis, the boy who moved in next door when I was six, was one of the first to chime in. "If they want to bring up old memories," he wrote, "let's ask them how many times your mom would leave you all alone?"

Another childhood friend recounted how my mom had told her parents she was dying of cancer and needed money. My friend said her parents noticed she didn't die, but she did have a new car.

Renee, who I used to ride with as a kid, wrote, "Some of us KNEW your mother."

My best friend from high school, Elizabeth, added: "I remember your mom very well. Who could forget the Christmas Tree Incident?"

"I feel like I owe every one of you an apology," I wrote after reading all those reality-check hugs from lifelong friends. "And somehow a fruitcake seems appropriate too."

"How many?" Cinnamon asked me.

"I'm up to three," I said.

"Six a night," she said.

"I know," I said.

It was a house rule that the girls at Cinnamon's had to sell a minimum of six drinks a night. You were supposed to hustle the guys and get them to buy you the twelve-dollar double, with the house getting six bucks and you getting the other half. They knew I didn't drink, and they knew I was underage, but it didn't matter. The bartender would secretly make mine a virgin, and the lie didn't sit well with me. I felt guilty making a guy buy a twelve-dollar Sprite and telling him, "Oooh, I love vodka."

Sometimes the guys would check, and if they caught you, they would get mad at you. I was already thinking long game, and that customer would then be someone who'd stand with his hands behind his back every time I danced. Worse, I just have a thing about liars, and I never wanted to be one.

This was bugging me more and more going into fall, and one October night a steady customer at the club got handsy with me. I batted him away and waved at the bouncer, thinking he would say something. Nothing. This jerk grabbed at me again. I yelled, this time so loud everyone heard me, which wasn't hard in a trailer titty bar. I looked right at the bouncer, imploring him to do something. He bit his bottom lip and glanced at the office.

He was too good a customer. I had worked there for nine months, lying to men about my Sprites to make the club an extra thirty-six dollars a night, but they wouldn't do anything to help me.

I got emotional and I went to the dressing room, stuffing all my things into a bag. I left Cinnamon's and I never went back. I am sorry to say that I left in anger, because I loved all those girls so much. Of all the women I have worked with over the years, they are the ones I still think about.

Right away, I knew who to call: the Gold Club.

The Gold Club was the nicest gentlemen's club in Baton Rouge. The guy on the phone said I could come in for an audition at two forty-five the next day, fifteen minutes before they opened. I met the managers, John and Larry, plus the floor guy, Casey.

The club was absolutely huge compared to Cinnamon's, but the guys were very nice and put me at ease. John had to go up in the DJ booth to cue up my Mötley Crüe song because the DJ wasn't even there yet. It was easier to do with nobody there, and I was confident I was a good dancer. That was always my saving grace: I could dance. I didn't just wander around the stage and make my butt clap.

"Do you want to start tonight?" asked John.

"Oh, I am going out tonight," I said. "I have plans."

"Well, do you want to work for a few hours and kind of get to know everybody?"

Right there they gave me a locker and I worked from three to eight. I had been nervous about the place being so much bigger than Cinnamon's, but I thought, *Well, this isn't too bad.*

Um, Stormy, that's because shit doesn't happen until after that. The next time I came in, I worked a night shift and was overwhelmed. There were forty-five girls working when I was used to six or seven a night, and there were three real stages instead of one the size of a bed. Upstairs had real VIP rooms, and you didn't have to sell drinks. If you wanted to do a private dance for someone in the back, you just had to raise your hand and the bouncer would run over with a box to stand on. Couldn't forget, the floor was lava there, too!

If you walked in at ten, you were going in cold, trying to get the attention of guys when you were one of many to choose from. But that's where the money was. There were three set shifts: three to eleven, eight thirty to two, and ten to two. Dancers had to pay a house fee for the two later shifts, with the last shift asking the highest house fee for the shortest time. A house fee is the "rent" you pay the club as a contractor occupying their space to offer your services. The same way hairstylists will often pay for their space at a salon. There was no fee if you came in at opening, because no girl wants to be there when it's three guys.

I wanted to avoid the house fee but wanted to maximize profit, so for the first five months, I worked the three-to-eleven shift, clocking out just as many girls were getting there. Then I got smarter and I would work a double, starting at three in the afternoon and not leaving until two in the morning. I could skip the house fee, establish my guys, and stay with them when the later girls rolled in.

I was a machine and got up to working six nights a week, with at least five of them being doubles. If I wasn't at work, I was spending money, and who wanted to do that? Plus, I truly *loved* dancing. I had regulars, and my favorite was Bear, this big huge guy who always wore Hawaiian shirts. His white hair and beard gave him the look of a polar bear. He was definitely a creature of habit, coming in every night at midnight after finishing his job as the nighttime manager of a Benny's Car Wash, and taking his usual spot on the top ledge to stay the last couple of hours. Once I saw he came in every night, I always made a point of dancing for him. Bear was never a big spender. He would tip a five onstage, and he only got table dances if it was a two-for-one, which they did every hour. Table dances were only ten dollars, but he always gave a twenty, and he always closed the night out with me. That meant Bear was good for between twenty-five and fifty dollars a night.

But late on a Friday or Saturday night, there's always a guy who wants to go into a VIP room and you can get six or seven hundred dollars, so the girls would ignore Bear to make that money. Not me—I would always give Bear the last dance of the night.

Girls would be like, "This guy wants to give you a hundred dollars for a table dance."

"No, I only dance for Bear."

"What's wrong with you?" was the constant refrain.

"He's twenty dollars every night," I said. *"Every week. Every month.* Do the math." He was sensitive about things, and why be rude to him one night to get two or three hundred dollars off this guy who I'm never gonna see again? It's the long game, and Bear taught me it.

Perhaps more than the money, doing the last dance every night with Bear meant that I would never go home in a bad mood. He wasn't some drunk tourist thinking he could do whatever he wanted because he threw money at me.

Another guy started coming in to the club named Brian. By then I had broken up with Andy. I had given up trying to fix his darkness. Brian was handsome and tall, so preppy that he didn't look like anyone I'd ever been with. But he was funny and we clicked in conversation. He was twenty-six, and we started dating February 7, 1998, a month before I turned nineteen.

Brian and I moved into a house we rented together, and we were very happy. We were so living the American dream that we even got a dog, a Sheltie we named Sasha.

Part of the American dream is making money. I am a firm believer in capitalism. And I noticed that the girls at the Gold Club who invested in breast implants got more tips. I was already a 36B, heading to a C, but I wanted to go bigger. There were three doctors in Baton Rouge who did everyone's boobs, so I started comparison-shopping at the club, asking the girls who they went to and deciding whose boob work I liked best.

I chose Dr. Charles Gruenwald, a suave-looking guy with prematurely gray hair and absolutely no bedside manner. When I went for the consultation, he came in the room and said, "Lemme look at them." *Phump,* off came my shirt and he was immediately hands-on, making judging grunts. I told him I wanted to go up to a 36D.

"Okay, okay," he said. He barreled through an explanation of his proposed procedure, then jotted down a price on a piece of scrap paper. "Gonna be this much," he said. "Let me know if you want it or not." And he walked out.

I almost didn't go back, but I decided to go ahead with it because he could put implants under the muscle, through incisions in my underarms. I scar really badly and wanted to avoid incisions under the breasts or on my nipples. Plus, this way I would be able to breastfeed if I ever chose to have a baby. Because they have to pop the muscle away from the bone, it's a much more involved and dangerous surgery; some doctors just won't do it. So, Dr. Grunts it was.

On a July morning in 1999, Brian drove me to the surgery and waited for me outside. I wasn't really nervous—I just wanted to get it over with. I had been working even more than usual, saving up for being out of commission at the club for about two weeks. The surgery was twenty-two hundred dollars, and I bet today it would be fifteen grand easy.

Because they go in through your upper body, I knew it would take a while for the swelling to go down and for the implants to settle. The muscle has to relax and you have to massage the area as part of the recovery. You measure how far your boobs have dropped by how many fingers you can fit between your breast and your collarbone. When I woke up from surgery, it was one finger, so my boobs were way up high.

They started to look good really quickly, and I was excited for the swelling to finally go down so I could wear all the cute 36D bras I'd bought from Victoria's Secret. But at the two-week mark, when most of the swelling was supposed to be gone, they were still huge. None of my new bras were fitting me, so I went to Victoria's Secret and they measured me.

"Honey, you're a triple D," the sweet lady told me.

I almost shit my pants. I went back to Dr. Grunts. "How big are my fucking tits?" I asked. He was supposed to give me a 450 cc's on one side and 475 on the other, because everybody's got one bigger than the other.

He hemmed, and hawed, clearly not wanting to tell me. Finally, he opened the chart and said, "You're 575."

I almost shit myself again.

"I filled them up till I liked them," he said with a shrug.

"You're a fucking asshole," I hissed.

"You are a very broad cavity with wide shoulders, and everyone who does that comes back and gets 'em bigger," he said. "They looked so good that I didn't want to cut you twice."

That's what stopped me from suing him, but I was a cartoon character until they settled.

It helped that I got a lot more tips. Instantly. Now I've gone on to win many Best Breasts trophies. And every time I accept one of those, I thank him by name. Best twenty-two hundred dollars I ever spent.

I also named my breasts because I love them so much. Thunder and Lightning. I've had the same implants since 1999—they're almost old enough to drink.

For the next two years, I continued to work at the Gold Club more than sixty hours a week. I was happy making money and saving up to buy a house. I had my regulars and I never did anything illegal, mainly because I was a good girl and also because I was hopelessly naïve.

The Gold Club was well known, so they would have feature dancers come in. A feature dancer is someone who is known for her pictorials or films. She can travel all over and draws her fan base to a club. She is paid by the club, keeps her tips, and when she performs—usually about two shows a night—the other house girls all stop because the feature is the star attraction.

When features were there, I made it my mission to talk to all of them, because I wanted to be one someday. Most of them seemed standoffish and cold, and I have now learned why. It's not necessarily the women being chilly, it's that clubs really hate when the features try to "recruit" or give their information to get their best house girls away.

And some of them were just bitches.

The first one to show me what was possible in feature dancing on an artistic level was Leslie Wells. She wasn't famous and didn't care about getting into magazines or movies—she was all about the theatricality of her shows. A green-eyed blonde from Chattanooga, she could have just coasted on her looks and boobs. But her shows were so much more than that—they were mini skits that embraced the fun and humor of taking off your clothes in front of everyone. As I started to think about how I would structure my own shows, I modeled them after hers. It's a strip club—it's okay to smile. She quit performing and now is a wonderful playwright with two kids. I was honored to go see her and buy the costumes from some of her best shows. She said she didn't want anyone to have them but me.

But the feature dancer who had the biggest impact on my life was Devon Michaels. A gorgeous, incredibly fit brunette, Devon was about ten years older than me and had a lot of success parlaying her centerfolds and covers into feature dancing and the best-body contest circuit. She gave me the number of the first photographer who ever shot me, Dan Sparks. I went to see him at his studio in Atlanta and he shot all my very first layouts in one day. Those pictures got me the covers of *D-Cup, Gent,* and *Hustler's Busty Beauties.* The magazines identified me just as Stormy or Stormy Waters, my short-lived nom de porn at twenty.

Devon didn't stop there. She believed in me and was so generous that she flew me to Tucson, Arizona, to meet Jacquie the Costume Lady, who still makes all my costumes to this day. Jacquie measured me and I bought my first five thousand dollars' worth of spangled-out feature costumes. You might think all I need is a bikini, but that's not how a real performer works. When you command a room—getting not just the audience's attention but earning their tips—you need to be a sort of one-woman circus. You're a ringmaster, clown, lion, tightrope walker, magician, and magician's assistant all in one. Your clothes have to tell a story, and like any story there have to be layers and reveals to keep people focused on you. There's a reason one of the first things I did when I planned out my act was to learn how to blow fire.

Devon came through with phone numbers of agents, and

using the pictorials and covers that came out that summer, I booked feature dancing gigs starting in September. My boyfriend Brian was always cool about me being a dancer—after all, it's how we met—but he didn't like the idea of having a live-in girlfriend he never saw. We decided to split, but it was completely amicable. I kissed Sasha good-bye and started life on the road.

I needed a roadie, so I asked one of the Gold Club's bouncers, Mac, if he wanted to come along. Mac had been a marine and was a big guy who could get volatile quickly. A bouncer should be looking to resolve all problems, but Mac could sometimes *start* problems in the name of protecting me.

Nowadays, I mostly fly everywhere, but back then I drove around in my Dodge Durango with a twelve-foot trailer full of my costumes. Living on the road before GPS, I learned how to use a map and figure out the best routes for time and scenery. Mac and I just went from place to place, and I learned so much in all the strip clubs. My reputation was good, and the same clubs would ask me to come back. I showed up on time, I was polite to the staff, and I think the biggest thing was that I didn't drink. A lot of the girls got messy and would need babysitting by the end of the night.

The summer of 2001, Mac and I were at the Cheetah club in Pompano Beach, Florida. We were hanging out in the dressing room between my two shows for the night. The DJ bombed in, coming in so hot that he hit his head on a low pipe.

"You gotta come onstage right now," he said.

"I thought I had twenty minutes," I said.

"Pantera just walked in."

Mac sat up. Pantera was my favorite band after Acid Bath, but they were definitely Mac's number one.

"It's their drum tech's birthday," said the DJ. "His name's Kat, and they wanna know if you can pull him up onstage."

"Of course!" Mac and I said at the same time. I did the show, pulling Kat up onstage to cover him in chocolate syrup. From Pantera, there was the drummer Vinnie Paul and bassist Rex Brown, along with Paul Gray from Slipknot, and Kerry King and a couple of other people from Slayer. And one more guy, a not particularly hairy tour manager they all inexplicably called Wookie. Mac got to meet them all, and he was in thrash metal heaven.

At the end of the night, the Cheetah closed and we actually stayed a little later to clean up my dressing room. (You see why clubs love me?) We got in my Dodge Durango to leave, and when we pulled around we saw the rock gods from inside sitting on the curb.

"What are they doing?" I asked Mac. "Should we offer them a ride?"

"They're fucking Pantera," said Mac. "They don't need a ride."

"Hey," I called out the window. "Do you guys need a ride?"

"Our cab hasn't shown up," said Vinnie.

"Where do you need to go?" I asked.

They told me what hotel it was, and I said, "Okay, get in." We had to lay the seats down to get everyone in the back. Once we were on the road, Vinnie Paul said, "Play something."

Mac and I had been listening to Mötley Crüe, so I pressed Play and "Shout at the Devil" filled the air. These six or seven guys all started singing along behind me, and we did, too.

When we got to the hotel, Vinnie said to me, "Can we buy you guys a drink?"

Before I could answer, Mac jumped in. "Yes!" We went to the hotel bar, which was probably supposed to be closed, but I would learn that when you're a rock group you can pay to keep stuff open. There were some groupies there, and Vinnie whispered in my ear, "I need you to do me a favor."

"Depends what it is," I said.

"There's this girl here who won't leave me alone," he said. "Will you sit on my lap and hold my hand and pretend we're together?"

I did, and we actually had a great time talking.

"Are you guys gonna come to the show tomorrow night?" he asked us. I didn't know there was one. Mac looked at me, mouthing a subtle "Please, please, please."

"Pssh, *yeah*," I said. "Of course."

The show was at the Sunrise Musical Theater in Miami, so I told Mac we could spend one extra night in Florida. Wookie gave us laminates, which are backstage passes that hang from lanyards. They're magic keys at concerts. It was the Reinventing the Steel tour, so we were backstage with Slayer, Static-X, and Sepultura. Pantera opened with "Hellbound" and closed with "Primal Concrete Sledge" before coming back for an encore of "Cowboys from Hell." There was this great moment right before the last verse when the lead singer, Phil Anselmo, who was screaming the whole show, said a very polite, "Thank you all for coming."

Then Vinnie said backstage, "Are you coming tomorrow night?"

We were. We followed them to Orlando, where they played

the Hard Rock. I realized I was following the band. It felt weird to be trailing them in my Durango with all my stuff. They liked having me around, so I sent Mac packing with my truck and trailer back to Louisiana, and I stayed on Pantera's bus for two weeks.

There were three buses, with Anselmo and his girlfriend Stephanie staying holed away by themselves on his own bus. Then there was the crew bus. And the bus I was on, which had Vinnie Paul and Wookie. It was the fun bus, a mix of the band and crew. Those two weeks were what got me addicted to the tour life. Waking up in a new city every day and sitting on the bus sharing stories with these great people.

It was *Almost Famous*. In fact, there was one morning that I got up from my bunk around 6 A.M. and went down to sit in the front lounge with the bus driver. Vinnie came down, then Grady the guitar tech—they probably hadn't even been to bed yet. I was watching the world go by out the window when they started singing "Tiny Dancer" to me, just like the band does on the bus in *Almost Famous*. A couple of others joined; these were metal guys serenading me with "Pretty eyed, pirate smile, you'll marry a music man." In the movie, teenage Patrick Fugit's character says to Kate Hudson's Penny Lane near the end of the song, "I have to go home." She holds up a hand to his face, like she's casting a spell. "You *are* home," she says.

We were this new circus family. Every night girls came on the bus. Some of the guys used to collect Polaroids of the girls, and it was my job to take the pictures. I took good shots, I have to say, because I genuinely wanted the girls to look their best for rock chick posterity. Some of them were crazy, though. One night a girl tried to steal the towel rack from the bus bathroom.

We had to tackle her. Another time these girls came on—one beautiful and one as ugly as her attitude. They kicked off the ugly one, but the pretty one wanted to stay. In fact, she wanted to leave with us. As soon as the bus started in the giant empty arena parking lot, one tiny set of headlights turned on in the distance. Then the car came at us like something out of *Christine*. Our driver floored it, but she kept coming and almost rammed the bus. She was screaming out the window, "Give me back my friend!" And the pretty one didn't want to go! Sorry. Maybe if you'd just been nicer.

When we got to Cleveland, Billy Corgan and the country singer David Allan Coe came to the show. Billy was standing next to me up front, singing along to every Pantera song but doing it in his Smashing Pumpkins voice. It was so surreal. There were a lot of pyrotechnics and concussive blasts in the show, and I had memorized the time from seeing the concert over and over. When I knew a loud noise was about to hit, I would elbow Billy and signal him to put his fingers in his ears. He was so cute about it. We all went to the Crazy Horse strip club after, and Billy came along. When the night was over, the back of Billy's Range Rover was blocked by a pole, and we had to move it so all the extra people we'd been collecting could get in the back. I was the only one sober enough to drive, so I got behind the wheel super cocky, but I accidentally put it in reverse and backed it right into a pole. He wasn't mad at all, and there was no physical damage—just to my ego.

I had decided Chicago would be where I left the circus. I needed to get back to work. We had a night off, so we got rooms at the Ritz. They'd wanted to stay at the Four Seasons, but the last time they were there Dimebag Darrell from Pantera threw a chair out the window and the band was banned. We got in at midmorning, and we went straight to bed. I was staying with Wookie and for some reason I fucked him. It was just a friend thing, but we passed out right after and slept all day.

We had a band dinner at this really nice steak house in the city, and the restaurant had a dress code that required jackets on the men. Fortunately, the restaurant loaned the guys some to wear. The rocker tour uniform was T-shirts, camo shorts, and combat boots—so imagine that topped with stuffy suit coats. We all strolled in like we were crashing the debutante ball, and they ended up getting so drunk. Kerry King from Slayer sat to my right, tattoos all over his bald head. Let the record show that throughout this whole ruckus, Kerry had impeccable table manners. He was the only one who knew which fork went with which dish.

There was a guy playing the harp, and at one point, Rex from Pantera went over and dropped a few hundreds in his bowl. He took the harp away and started playing it like a bass. I was just amazed they didn't kick us out. Maybe Kerry's good manners saved us.

After one last concert, it was time for me to go back to my own tour. My friend Exotica and her roadie husband, Vinnie, were throwing a Fourth of July party at their house in a residential area outside Chicago. Exotica was a gorgeous Latin feature dancer, and she said I could stay with her until Mac arrived with my Durango and trailer. "My friends will drop me off in the morning before the party," I told her. "I can help set up."

We partied all night in Chicago, and at 6 A.M., our huge tour bus rolled into Exotica's white-picket-fence neighborhood. We parked, and the bus heaved a sigh of air brakes that I am sure woke the whole neighborhood, because suddenly people were all at their front doors. Exotica and her husband came out, too, staring with their mouths open.

Pantera and all my friends got off the bus to help me get my stuff out of the bay. Each gave me one last hug.

I walked up to Exotica. "Who are your friends?" she asked me, dumbfounded.

"They're the best," I said. "The best."

Mac and I started a romance on the road, and as we became more of a couple, he would get jealous. We fought a lot, and sometimes it got physical. There was a night I climbed through the window of a bathroom I'd locked myself in to get away from him. I wasn't having that, so I fired him and broke up with him all at once. We're cool now, but back then we just weren't good together.

I found Jay, a smaller guy who wasn't there for security but was great as a roadie. He could drive twenty-four hours without stopping and could size up a club within a minute of walking in. He was a bass player, and I have a thing for bass players, so I fell for him, too.

I'd clocked two years of feature dancing and was killing myself driving all over. I was making a hundred dollars a show before tips and doing fifteen shows a week. The problem was that I had topped out on rate. I'd done just about every magazine except *Penthouse* and *Playboy*. And the only way to bump your rate up after you top out is to do films. Devon Michaels, who opened so many doors for me, was in the same boat. She called me one day and told me, "I'm going to go to L.A. I've decided to do porn."

"Oh, my God, wow," I said. I didn't have any negative views of people who worked in the adult entertainment industry. In fact, I loved porn and had a collection of DVDs. This was before the internet made porn so readily accessible—you had to want it to see it.

"You should come with me," she said.

"I've never . . ."

"I'll buy your ticket," she said. "Will you come with me?"

Sold. We both flew to L.A. on May 1, 2002. Right off the plane that very first day, she was booked to do an all-girl sex scene for *Makin' It,* a film for Wicked Pictures. It starred Stephanie Swift playing a young singer trying to break into show business. Wicked was actually my favorite of the various movie studios. They made very cinematic films that blended action and story, many of which were remakes of popular mainstream films or send-ups of genres. My favorite film was *Dream Quest,* a 2000 Wicked production starring Jenna Jameson as a modern woman drawn into a fairy tale. It was directed by Brad Armstrong, who would be shooting Devon that day. Brad was also a performer, and I found him incredibly hot.

Devon asked if I wanted to come along, and of course I did. That day I learned what I still tell people: "You don't want to go to set. It's going to ruin porn for you forever." It's not that it's somehow degrading or gross—it's that there's nothing spontaneous about it whatsoever. Everyone is there to do a job. I saw this way up close right away, because Brad said I could sit in a little closet on set, just three feet from the four-way but still out of the shot. It was the film's star Stephanie Swift, Nicole Sheridan, my friend Devon, and another girl pretending to be in the dressing room of a *Coyote Ugly*–type bar. They're dancers and they're counting their tips, which naturally leads to getting out dildos.

These four girls were going at it like they were inventing girl-on-girl rough sex. The grunts, the cries, the "yeah, yeah, yeahs." One girl was using a double-ended dildo to fuck another one doggy-style while also thrusting the opposite end into herself. Devon was helpfully spreading the ass cheeks of the receiver while getting fucked with another dildo. It takes a village.

Stephanie was going, "Unh unh unh unh" at the top of her lungs when Brad said, "Cut."

They all broke character, relaxing their bodies with double-headed dildos still inside them.

"Do you think the weather is gonna be good this week?" Stephanie asked, as the camera guy switched tapes. Back then you had to do that for every twenty minutes of film.

"I think so," said Nicole, just as nonchalant. "I don't think there's rain coming, so it might just stay humid."

The tech said, "Ready," and they were right back at it.

"Oh, God, yes, yes, yes, yes!" screamed Nicole, in time with each thrust of a dildo.

After a while, Brad said, "Cut. I want to move the lighting." While the men on the crew saw to that, the girls checked their nails.

"Is anyone gonna be at that party Friday?" said Nicole.

"Oh, it's so far out," said Stephanie. "I don't know if—"

"Action," said Brad.

"Yeah, like that!" yelled Stephanie, falling right back into

heavy-breathing rhythm. "Just like that, you fucker! Oh, God, oh, God!"

On set, you're not just breaking the fourth wall. You're pissing on it, then knocking it over with a bulldozer. But I still found it interesting, so when I went back the next day I agreed to shoot a scene as a clothed extra. They did my makeup and it was the very first time I'd ever had it professionally done. And it was the first time I ever wore false eyelashes.

"These are so heavy," I said, my eyelids drooping down and then flashing up as I got used to them. *How do you people do it?* I wondered. Now I can put them on while driving!

I got on camera and these little murmurs went up in the crew. Jake Jacobs, the camera operator, called Ric Rodney, the lighting guy, to look.

"Hunh," they said, each turning their heads. Ric came over, adjusted a light near me, and Jake nodded.

"What?" I said.

"Don't take this the wrong way," said Jake. "You're pretty, but you're *beautiful* on camera."

I didn't take it the wrong way. Jake would shoot every single movie I would do. Ric is still my guy when it comes to lighting my films.

Brad Armstrong came over to me. "Do you do movies?"

"Well, no," I said. "But I love them."

"I think the owner of the company would like to meet you," he said. "Maybe talk to you about a contract."

I didn't even know there was such a thing. When you do a contract, you work exclusively for that company and have job security and a company promoting you like the old MGM studio system. Jenna Jameson had been a contract girl for Wicked.

I knew Devon really wanted a contract and didn't want to be a freelancer.

"Oh, I don't know," I said. "I'm just here with Devon. Isn't Devon incredible? She—"

"We should go out tonight and get dinner," Brad said. When I didn't immediately answer, he added: "The three of us."

"Okay."

"Where do you wanna go?" he asked.

"I want to see the Sunset Strip," I said, which made him burst out laughing because that is such a touristy thing to want to do. "I need to see the Whisky a Go Go, 'cause that's where Mötley Crüe played and they lived above it."

"Fair enough," he said.

That night Brad picked us up in a convertible Camaro that had the Wicked logo across it. It was the Wicked pace car, and the company was printing money at that point. We went to the Saddle Ranch Chop House, which has a rock-and-western atmosphere. I rode the mechanical bull, of course, and I won five hundred dollars for managing to stay on. Brad told me later that as he was watching me ride the bull he was like, in a villain voice, "I must be in her."

The three of us went back to his house, and the whole time I'm thinking, *This is going to be two firsts.* My first threesome, and my first one-night stand. Adding to that, this was the first time I'd ever had sex with someone who I considered a man. Someone who wasn't my age. Brad is about fourteen years older than me—and he owns a house. It didn't get more adult to me than that.

We were sitting in a circle on his bed, kissing and making out. Brad pulled his dick out, and it was the biggest dick I'd ever seen up to that point. Now, in Pornland, I can now tell you it is very average. But it was the biggest penis *I'd* ever seen.

I fell backward off the bed and hit my head. "There's no way that's gonna fit!" I yelled. (Reader, it fit.)

Brad offered to help me meet with the owner of Wicked, and I took him up on it. But first I was set to go along with Devon, who was shooting a girl-girl scene in *American Girls: Part Two* for a company called Sin City. The second girl canceled, and Devon panicked because she was scared to work with someone she didn't know.

I'm a girl's girl, so I got roped into it. The premise of this girl-girl scene was typical porn: We are hiking when my friend sprains her ankle out on the trail. I give her a shoulder to lean on, and when that doesn't fully do the job, I comfort her with my vagina. The film was directed by Michael Raven, who later came to Wicked as a director. The cameraman on set that day was François Clousot, who I just shot with the other day, and the makeup artist was a girl named Shelby Stevens, who left the business but I swear I was just texting a few minutes ago. Once you click with me, I'm with you for life.

We shot in Dry Gulch Ranch, this rocky, desert location in the Santa Monica Mountains of West Malibu. There were all these terms they use in porn that I didn't know. The first was "Wildlife!" They yelled that out, and it just means there's a bug or creature wandering onto the set. They weren't kidding: There was a scorpion wandering the set that day, and I saw my first tarantula.

Then I heard Michael say, "Okay, thirty seconds to build up to a FIP."

I froze. "What's a FIP?" I yelled. "I don't know if I do that!"

It's a fake orgasm, a "Fake Internal Pop." The term is used in soft-core filmmaking because you can't show guys coming in those films, so it's simulated. Usually it's for boy-girl scenes, obviously, but it's also used for girls.

The next day, a Friday, Brad made good on his offer to introduce me to the owner of Wicked. He seemed interested, but he's not someone who really shows his cards. I was scheduled to take a red-eye back to Baton Rouge the next day, and Devon was flying out for a dance booking. I was staying at Brad's—so much for a one-night stand—and right before he took me and Devon to the airport, he pulled me aside.

"If you decide to stay, I could make you a star," he said. "Whether or not you sign with Wicked, someone will sign you. And you will go on to make a minimum fifteen thousand dollars a month."

"What?" I said, immediately doing the math. One hundred eighty thousand dollars a year sounded like a gold mine.

"I'll help you if you want me to," he said. "But this is kind of your shot."

We got to LAX, which was fucking terrifying to someone who'd never really been by herself in a big city. Brad got my carry-on out of the back of the Camaro, and I said good-bye. I promised I'd be back someday. I could tell he didn't believe me.

Devon's flight was first, so I waited with her until she left. I thanked her for the millionth time for always doing so much for me. And then it was just me, all alone. I sat at the gate for my flight to Baton Rouge. I looked at the sign and sighed. They were boarding first class. I was way in the back. I looked at my bag, then the Baton Rouge sign again.

I heard Brad's voice in my head. "This is kinda your shot."

This is my shot, I thought. I knew I was only going to get one.

I grabbed my bag and I walked out of the airport. I wasn't even old enough to rent a car, I didn't have a credit card, and I didn't have any money. I called the only number that I had in L.A.

Brad Armstrong answered on the first ring.

"I just walked out of the airport," I said.

He gave me the name of a Mexican restaurant and bar he was heading to in Calabasas. "Take a cab there and I'll meet you."

It was a Cinco de Mayo party, and some of the biggest names in the porn industry were there. Brad paid my fare, then walked me around, introducing me to all these amazing people. I went home with him that night and we lived together as a couple for the next fourteen months. I left everything else behind, and I had my car shipped from Baton Rouge.

Because he liked me, Brad thought Wicked would probably sign me. But he also knew that no matter how respected he was in the business, I had to at least shoot a lead before Wicked would make me a contract star. With his clout, he walked me right in to meet the directors at the companies that he wanted me to work with. I never had an adult agent, and I never had an adult manager. I can hear you thinking, "Oh, here's where she gets screwed." Quite the opposite. I am the first to admit I was handed this golden ticket. I was in the right place at the right time and I grew the right set of balls in the moment so that I would not miss my shot.

I never had to climb the ranks or do the hard stuff. Or do scenes without a condom. I've been in the adult industry all this time and I've never had a dirty test, which is when you test positive for chlamydia or gonorrhea. I don't have herpes, which is crazy, because a lot of people do, especially in the business. And it's because Brad took me by the hand and walked me into the office of people who he trusted and he knew would take care of me. I only did top-shelf projects, and I was usually the lead. I know that was a source of a lot of jealousy for people who had really done their due diligence and had worked their way up. Later, when *Adult Video News* nominated me for Performer of the Year—which is like a Best Actress Oscar in our industry— they asked the people nominated to do on-camera interviews that they teased until the end of the awards show.

In the interview, they asked me, "Why do you think you deserve to win Performer of the Year?"

"I fucking *don't*," I said. "I'm embarrassed to be here—I didn't earn this. There are girls who are literal sexual acrobats and have been in the trenches. I've been a cream puff." They never nominated me again. That's my problem, I'm too honest. But I think the girls in that room could look at me and say, "At least the bitch is honest."

When I started doing films, Brad gave me some advice. "You should stick to doing girl-girl and solo stuff at first," he said. "Pace yourself. Because if Wicked decides to give you a contract, they're gonna want your first boy-girl." Brad also wanted to be the one to do my first boy-girl scene with me. He wasn't giving that up.

When an opportunity arose to do a scene with him as a lead in a Wicked film, I took it. For *Heat*, Brad wrote me as Charlotte, a Louisiana vixen—hmmph—who plots to steal eighty-seven thousand dollars from a drifter con artist whose car breaks down in my little town. I found doing a boy-girl scene to be easier for me than girl-girl. Just logistically, when it comes to kissing another woman, you've got two sets of lashes hitting, the lipstick all over the place. Guys usually have no ego with me, whereas girls . . . Let's be honest, this is a business where your income and popularity are directly related to how pretty you are.

By the time I did *Heat,* I was blonder. I'd noticed that the head of Wicked preferred blondes, and the more blond I got, the more work I got. Finally, I went fully blond, and it's amazing what blond hair and big boobs instantly do, by the way. Everyone thinks you're stupid, but they sure want you around. Sure enough, two months into my career, Wicked signed me and I had to finalize a stage name. My initial thought was Stephanie Storm, but they said it was too close to Stephanie Swift, another actress.

"Why don't you keep Stormy?" the boss said. "There's never been a Stormy, and it just suits you."

Going with Stormy felt weird. Brad was born Rod Hopkins. Marilyn Monroe was Norma Jean Mortenson. If I had to be this larger-than-life character onscreen, could I really do it as Stormy? But I went with it, and chose Daniels as a last name, a tribute to a Jack Daniel's ad I saw that called it "a Southern favorite." You can take the girl out of her Dodge Durango and hitch-trailer . . .

Magazines were really huge back then, and Brad told me I needed to start meeting photographers. "You can shoot with them and increase your profile without saturating the video market," he said. "Are there any photographers that you know?"

"Not in L.A.," I said. "The only photographer that I know by name out here isn't interested in shooting me."

"How do you know?" he asked.

"Because I've submitted Polaroids for years and they've never even responded."

"Well, who's that?" he asked. "I can't imagine anyone not wanting to shoot you."

"You have to say that because we're fucking," I said. "Her name's Suze Randall."

"Suze?" he said. "Let's go to her house right now."

"What? You know Suze?"

"She shoots me all the time," he said. "She'll shoot you."

Suze Randall is a legend in photography, not just for being so talented, but for being a trailblazer. Born in England, she was initially a model, then became *Playboy*'s first female staff photographer and also one of the first women to direct porn. I was so nervous for the entire ride to her place, a thirty-acre ranch outside Malibu. As we approached, I saw she had horses, and my heart leapt a little.

She greeted us in riding pants, a dirty shirt, and a Q-tip shock of white hair. She immediately grabbed at Brad's crotch. "Did you bring me a new little sluttie?" she asked, her demented singsong British accent making her sound like some horny headmistress. I was instantly in love. "Ohhhh," she purred. "We need to get her on the calendar right away."

The next time I was at the ranch, we shot in her studio. Before Suze even showed up, there were hours of prep work on lighting and wardrobe. Emma Nixon, a former model, did my makeup, and once again I was blinking from the weight of fake lashes. Finally, Suze came in and sat on a skateboard so she could quickly roll back and forth to get the angles.

"That's right, show 'em your pink little twattie," she said. "That's a good little piggy. Piggy, piggy, piggy." She could never get away with that now, but after I was over the initial horror, I fell deeper in love. Especially when I saw the finished product.

She went on to shoot me fifty times and got me my first layout in *Penthouse*.

Once again, Brad had opened doors for me. I began tagging along to all of his sets to watch him direct. He was great at what he did, but writing all those scripts didn't seem to be his favorite part, so he sometimes fell behind. We were sitting in bed together and he was grimacing at the screen.

"I could write you a script," I said.

He gave me such a side-eye and ignored me.

"No, I'm a writer," I said.

He laughed at me. Just fully laughed in my face. *Now* I understand because I have had a thousand people say those sentences to me and not one of them gave me something remotely usable. He'd been pestered for years by people saying, "I have an idea," thinking it's so easy to write a porno. I get it and forgive him now, but in the moment? No.

"Go fuck yourself!" I yelled. I went and got my laptop, then stamped my feet down the hallway to the other room to start working on a script. I gave it to him a couple of days later. The look on his face is forever burned into my brain, and I go to it when I am blocked in writing. It was a look of *Holy shit, she actually can write*. He bought it from me right then and there for seven hundred dollars. He shot the film and then knew exactly how to tease another one out of me. "Think you can do it again?"

I wrote another script, and another script, and another. He was in heaven because he didn't have to write. I was in heaven because I got to write and got *paid* to write. Then the other directors at Wicked, who were now Jonathan Morgan and Michael Raven, wanted to buy scripts. I started writing for them. The word got out in the industry that I was a really good writer, at which point Wicked put the kibosh on that and added writing to my contract. So now I was a contract star and contract writer. I could write for anybody in the company but not outside it. After that, I wrote every Wicked movie that I starred in.

When I write, the movie plays in my head as I work. I see it as I write, and because of my memory, when it's time for the shoot I remember every beat and angle of the film I envisioned when I first wrote the script in longhand. This isn't a knock on anyone at Wicked, because they're all fantastic directors, but it was like I had already watched my movie in my head and I hated not seeing it exactly that way on the screen. It could be as simple as imagining the girl wearing a pink dress, not a yellow one, but some of it was bigger changes, and I started to get in huge fights with Brad.

"I'm just gonna have to have you stop coming to set," he yelled at me after one too many objections from me.

"You're ruining my vision!" I yelled. Oh, gosh, that sentence haunted me for years. "Don't ruin her vision" became a running joke in the company. I got in a huff, let's call it a hufflepuff, and I went in to the owner of Wicked and convinced him that I knew how to direct. Just once I wanted to see if I could take something from my head, to paper, to life. And he said yes. Keep in mind they were still making money to burn if they wanted to. No one could afford to take this risk these days, but back then a thirty-five-thousand-dollar gamble to appease the star was nothing.

So now I had to do it.

I wrote a script called *One Night in Vegas* with Kaylani Lei, one of our contract stars, in mind. The first day on set, I sat down at the monitor and realized that I'd done the blocking and told everyone what to do, but I didn't know how to start. Everybody was listening and looking at me and I was like, *Oh shit*.

Jake Jacobs, the cameraman on my first day as an extra and then my first Wicked film, was standing right there by me with the camera.

"What do I say now?" I whispered to him.

He didn't blow my cover or rat me out. He whispered, "You say, 'Rolling, speeding.'"

"Rolling!" I yelled. "We're speeding."

He waited a beat, then whispered, "Now say 'Action.'"

I swallowed.

"You can do it," he whispered.

"Action," I said in a voice only loud enough for him to hear.

"Say it louder."

"Action!"

Thank you, Jake. Halfway through that day, we were shooting a party scene with a bunch of people coming in and out. Of course, I had to make my first movie as difficult as possible with extras and moving parts. As I was standing at the top of this staircase looking down to figure out blocking and timing, I suddenly realized that everyone was looking at me and I was commanding a room of twenty people. I was twenty-two years old, and I had the epiphany that so many people go through life never having that moment where you can say, "This is it. This is what I was born to do." And I've been drunk with power ever since.

One Night in Vegas turned out great, and when the owner of the movie company saw the finished film, directing was quickly added to my contract. Now I was a Wicked contract star, writer, and director.

———

"Who the hell is that?" I whispered to Jessica Drake. We were on set for a movie I wrote called *Highway*. We were Wicked's most successful contract stars and had hit it off. I had written us a buddy movie just so we could have fun together. It was based on *Thelma & Louise*, and I chose Michael Raven to direct. We were shooting at Four Aces Movie Ranch, a set you've seen in a hundred movies, with a fifties-style diner and motel. It's an hour northeast of L.A. in the middle of nowhere, so if you're there, you're there for a reason.

"One of them's got a camera," said Jessica. "They press?"

"I'm gonna find out," I said.

The guys had walked over to Lyle and Jim, who were Wicked's in-house art department. They were hugging, all buddy-buddy.

"Who are they?" I said, not looking at them.

"This is Keith Munyan and Dean Keefer," Lyle said. "Keith is shooting the box cover."

Now, I am a creature of habit, as you know. I don't like change. Brad Willis had shot the stills for my previous box covers and publicity. I didn't know that Brad had moved on to doing more design than photography, I just knew that it looked like Lyle and Jim had hired their friends to shoot our box cover. I was sure they sucked, and I told Jessica as much when I walked back.

"I don't really like people photographing me when I haven't seen their work," she said. "How do we know he's not gonna try to sell the photos?" She was older than me and had been in the business longer. I always trusted her opinion and admired her business acumen.

"You're right," I said. "He might make me look like shit. I need to see his test photos. Let him audition." Or quit.

I sat for Keith that first day in the corner of the diner set in the ranch. I sat in a booth across from a weathered bumper sticker on the wall reading AMERICA: LOVE IT OR LEAVE IT. Keith is a talker, and I immediately picked up a strong Louisiana accent. I resolved not to acknowledge it or speak to him to reveal mine.

He showed me the first shot on his camera. I smiled and yelled to Jessica through the window. "Okay, we're gonna be nice to this guy now," I said. "We're gonna keep him."

"What part of Louisiana are you from?" I asked.

"How did you know?" Keith asked.

"I'm from Baton Rouge," I said.

"I'm from the swamps."

We laughed, kindred spirits. Keith and Dean were in their forties, partners in business and in life. They're both good-looking guys, and Keith was a model before he was a photographer. When I become friends with someone, I am all in. I practically say, "We're gonna be friends now. We're gonna get bunk beds and do activities."

I had a shoot coming up, just some content for my website. My photographer canceled and I immediately thought of Keith. I did a day alone with him, and they were the best pictures ever taken of me up to that point. Pretty much instantly, I told Wicked and anyone else who wanted photos, "No one else is allowed to shoot me." From that day forward, just about every professional photo ever taken of me was by Keith. He had never shot layouts for magazines, and many editors understandably didn't trust someone they hadn't worked with before. But I told them that if they wanted me they had to hire Keith Munyan. I didn't care if it was *Penthouse,* or Spencer Gifts doing my calendar. He's with me.

My bond with Keith and Dean proved to be even stronger than friendship. I became so close to them that they finished raising me. I call them my gay dads, and I mean that. If my biological father gets to call himself my dad, then I sure as hell get to say who my real dads are.

When Brad Armstrong and I broke up, it was Keith who took care of me. I could see it coming, but I didn't anticipate just how he would do it. Brad was often hard to read and not really affectionate. He would build a little wall of pillows between us on the bed when we slept because my instinct is to cuddle. I also knew that the women he was with had a shelf life of one year. I was pushing it at fourteen months.

One day he mentioned offhand that he was taking Jessica Drake wardrobe shopping for her new movie. I didn't think much of it, but it put me in the mood to check out clothes that I might want some of my stars to wear. I went to the Westfield Topanga Mall, and just like that day that I saw my high school boyfriend holding hands with that pretty girl at the coffee shop, there were Brad and my buddy Jessica, holding hands as they went up the escalator. I could tell by the way they were acting that this wasn't new.

I didn't chase them up the escalator. Ever the director, I wanted the confrontation scene to be just right. I ran to another escalator and went up just so I could do a sneak attack on them.

"Well, well, well," I said, "this is some interesting wardrobe shopping. *How long have you guys been fucking?*" Jessica said nothing and couldn't even look at me. I was as hurt about being betrayed by my friend as by my boyfriend cheating. I wanted to kill her, and Brad had to talk me down. And I left.

In the car, I called my dad Keith. He told me to come over right away. When I got there, I hugged him. "It's now official," I said with a sigh. "You're my favorite person. There's no competition."

Keith remained my favorite person, even when I woke up accidentally married to someone I'd dated all of two weeks.

I was still heartbroken by Brad and Jessica when I started dating a director named Pat Myne, who I knew by his real name, Bart Clifford. He was in his late thirties and a really nice guy, and had been married to another performer, Shelbee Myne, before divorcing in 1999. Bart and I had been seeing each other for two weeks when we were both in Las Vegas for an adult entertainment convention in 2003. That night in Vegas, I did something very uncharacteristic: I drank. Which is to say that I tried to drown my sorrow about Brad and Jessica in a vat of tequila. The next morning, I woke with my head pounding and my makeup artist friend Christine standing over me holding a marriage license.

"What the fuck is this?" she screamed.

I didn't remember, but I have since seen photos of Bart and me at a drive-through chapel. I had pink stripes in my hair, which speaks to my insanity at the time. I found Bart in the hotel, and we had to get used to the idea that we were married.

We never really did get used to that idea. I made a go of it because he had a preteen daughter from a previous relationship, Taylor, who he saw quite a bit of. I grew to love her, but Bart and

I were only together a year before we decided it was best to split and that what happened in Vegas really just should have stayed in Vegas.

Christine, my friend who informed me I was married, was always urging me to talk to my mother. She was otherwise a very sensible person, but I knew that idea was nuts. But Christine had a very good and healthy relationship with her mother and her grandmother. They have been close her whole life. She couldn't get her head around the fact that I wouldn't talk to my mom. Society also drills into you the importance of family. "But that's your mother," we hear. "That's blood!" No matter how toxic it is, we're supposed to just drink the poison, and maybe this time they won't let you down. There is so much pressure to honor blood ties, when really my chosen family is the people who have always done right by me.

But there was no convincing Christine. One day we were in New Orleans for work. I was competing in the Gold G-String Awards at the Penthouse Club, which had taken over the Gold Club space. I was there with my roadie Scotty and my stepdaughter, Taylor, who was about twelve and off school for spring break. I wanted her to see New Orleans, and I had all my days free during the trip. Christine was there when my mom's number popped up as an incoming call. I recoiled from the phone, but she insisted I pick it up. When I did, my mom told me she had seen an advertisement about me and the show. It's one of the biggest feature dancer contests of the year, and she wanted to come see me. She had seen my show, showing up when I was in

Baton Rouge and New Orleans; she loved the reactions and she told everyone in the bar she was my mother. "Don't you give my baby a dollar!" she'd scream. "You give her a twenty!" Any disapproval she had of my life paled in comparison to the attention it brought her.

I initially said no to her attending out of instinct, but Christine convinced me I should give her a chance. I called her back to lay some ground rules before she drove the fifty minutes from Baton Rouge to New Orleans. "You can't stay the night, okay?" I said. "We have two hotel rooms and all my costumes. Me, Christine, and Taylor are sharing a room, and my roadie Scotty has his own room. With all of the makeup, all of the costumes—there's no room in this La Quinta Inn for you."

"I'll sleep on the floor," she said.

"No, no, you cannot stay," I said. If I had said, "Don't wear black," she would insist she was on her way to a funeral and needed to. She only wanted something when I wouldn't give it to her. But I was adamant, because I didn't know how much exposure I wanted my stepdaughter to have to my mother. Or *me* when I'm around my mother. I needed to be able to say, "Okay, we're going to bed, you can leave now."

I was suspicious as soon as I saw she arrived with a bag.

"What's that for?"

"Oh, you know, just in case."

I made eye contact with Christine, who smiled. My mom was on her best sweetie-pie behavior. Butter wouldn't melt.

"Sheila's so nice," Christine told me while my mom wandered around the room, clearly scoping out a place to thwart me and stay the night. "What's the big deal?"

I turned when my roadie Scotty walked into the room. It had never occurred to me to mention to my mom that he was black. "Scotty," I said, "this is my mom, Sheila."

"Ooooooooh," she said. "My baby's made it. She has her own black man."

All I heard was a thud as Christine dropped something behind me. I watched the look on Scott's face change from certain he had misheard to angry to "Who is this woman?"

I was prepping for my show that has this big huge Smokey the Bear as a comic thing. In the show, I light a campfire and he comes out and says, "Only you can prevent forest fires." And he "pees" on it with a fake penis. Well, TSA had taken my fake penis out of my bag and kept it. I was trying to make one with a ketchup bottle, but we needed something dark to cover it so it wouldn't be bright red or yellow on stage. None of us had dark socks—except my mom. She gave us one, we cut a hole in it, and it worked. I was super grateful and I gave her a pair of my socks in return.

"You saved the day," Christine told my mom. I winced internally, knowing this would just feed her ego. But then I wondered why I couldn't just let my mother have this moment. Maybe Christine was right.

The show went great, but I could see her in the audience and I noticed she was having a couple of drinks. My mother does not drink, so I knew what she was up to: this was a manipulative tactic, because then it would mean she couldn't drive. When she said just that, I was very direct. "We're all going to Denny's and you're gonna eat some fucking pancakes and drive your fucking ass home."

"Oh, I could just lay down in your bed until you get back."

"Nope," I said. "No."

The Denny's was attached to the hotel and we got there at two o'clock in the morning. I first went up and checked on Taylor, who was sleeping soundly. I went back down and there were a bunch of other performers there, too. We got a bunch of tables together and all sat to eat like a family.

Except my mother, who sat sniffling, going into baby talk. I had forgotten she would do that to people when I was little. She started to cry and said, "I don't know why Stormy doesn't like me."

She was putting on a performance, and I knew it, but people who didn't know her as I did were horrified and thought I was terrible. Everyone but Scotty, who could see right through her. Halfway through the meal, she upped the drama of her scene with an exaggerated cry to the heavens. She stopped short, looked for reactions, and then continued.

"Are you okay?" asked Christine.

"Don't even talk to her," I said. "She can sit there and cry."

Everyone just wanted to leave, but I said, "Nope, I am just gonna sit here and finish my waffle." Never have I sipped orange juice so slowly. Finally, I finished and the four of us headed to the stairs so she could get her bag and go home. I told her there was no room in my room because I had Taylor in my bed and Christine was in the other.

"You can sleep in Scotty's room and use a pullout bed," I said. I saw his head swivel, but I knew she wouldn't take the bait.

"I'm a fine Southern woman," she said. "I do not share rooms with black men."

"Get your shit," I hissed. "And then leave. You are not staying."

The real her came through and she began screaming at me,

calling me a cunt. Lights started going on in the hotel, so Christine slipped in to get her bag. I took my mother back downstairs to the parking lot to make sure she left. The hotel shared a huge parking lot with a mall, so there was this vast expanse of parking spaces. She had parked near where they were doing construction, and there was a trailer with a temporary fence around it.

She got in her car, still screaming at me. "You stole my sock, you cunt! I wish I'd aborted you!"

"Okay," I said dismissively. "Okay. I wish you had, too. You have a good night, now."

She took off in her car, but her rear bumper caught the end of the chain-link fence around the small construction site. The last thing I saw of my mother that night was the taillights of her Ford Escort going across the parking lot, dragging this chain-link fence that's sparking on the asphalt. "I'm gonna go off the bridge and kill myself and it will be all your fault!" she screamed out the window. "You stole my sock!"

I went back upstairs and crept into the room. Taylor was asleep. Christine sat on her bed, bathed in light from the moon and the streetlights of the parking lot.

"I fucked up," she said.

"Yes," I said, "yes, you did. I told you. It's okay, you have to see it to believe it."

"I'll never—" she said, cutting herself off. "Yeah. Sorry I pressured you."

"Well, payback's a mother," I said with a laugh. "Take it from me."

I auditioned on a whim, not really that invested in breaking into mainstream films. It was late 2004, and Jonathan Morgan, a fellow contract director at Wicked Pictures, told me he had seen an ad for an open audition for a movie starring Steve Carrell.

"It's called *The 40-Year-Old Virgin*," he said.

"Can't help you there," I joked.

"They are looking for girls comfortable with nudity to play a stripper type," he said.

"Ding ding ding! I know that girl."

I went down to the casting cattle call in L.A. just because I thought it would be something new to do. I read for it, playing up the comedy of the writing, and I got a callback. But when I went in for the second reading, they warned me the scene had completely changed.

"Are you comfortable with your character also doing a scene in a fake porn?" asked the very nice casting agent.

"I only have a problem with the fake part," I joked. "Why shoot a fake porn when I can just get you the license to one of my real porns?"

"Oh, well . . ."

"That would actually help, because it would help sell my movie, and then you guys don't have to shoot something extra."

"That actually makes a whole lot of fucking sense," said the agent.

I got the part, and they got to use *Space Nuts,* a sci-fi send-up I starred in, but directed and written by Jonathan, who had given me the heads-up about the part. Production started in January, and I met the director, Judd Apatow. He was incredibly polite and focused on the work, but his set was fun. It felt like an extended family, and each time I met someone new, I got the backstory on how they joined the fold. I particularly hit it off with the on-set producer Shauna Robertson, who had met Judd while executive-producing Will Ferrell's *Anchorman: The Legend of Ron Burgundy,* which she got because she did such an amazing job producing *Elf.* Shauna is this little California chick with honey-blond hair and such great energy. She's exacting, and even if she has ten different to-dos going in her head, she has this calmness to her. There's never a moment when she is not drawing you in with a sense of "Isn't this cool that we get to do this?"

My second day on set, she came to me with a proposition. "There's this new guy on set who's known Judd for years," she said. "He comes from television, but this is his first real role in a film. We want to prank him. You can say no—totally no big deal, but it's going to be epic."

"I'm in," I said. Nothing makes me happier than pranking someone. Or doing something where the guaranteed outcome is "epic."

"Okay," she said, grabbing my arm with excitement. "So, he knows there's a famous porn star on set named Stormy, and we want to tell him you're a big fan of his from his TV show. The story is that we need you to come back to do this reshoot but you said you'd only come back if you could meet him."

"Got it," I said.

"You've insisted he go to your trailer and take a picture with you," Shauna said. "When he gets there, we want you in a bathrobe with champagne. Be, like, super creepy."

"I can do super creepy."

"We had the tattoo lady on set make a fake tat to put on your boob. *It's of his face.* When you make him really uncomfortable, we want you to whip out your boob and ask, 'Do you like my tattoo?' We're going to have cameras up to tape the whole thing."

"Even more in."

"Oh, God, I love you. His name is Seth Rogen and the show you loved is *Freaks and Geeks.*"

Seth was hysterically awkward in the face of crazy me, and the prank went so well they made it a DVD extra on the unrated version of *40-Year-Old Virgin* titled "My Date with Stormy." Because I did that, I got to join the family. They didn't even hold auditions for *Knocked Up* when they needed someone to do half-naked physical comedy with Seth and Paul Rudd. They went straight to the source. "I just remember that she was very smart and really strong and funny," Judd told the *Daily Beast* in March of this year, "to the point where we kept asking her to do silly things in our movies."

Judd was awesome, but I owe my movie education to Shauna. She let me tag along to all her sets, films such as *Superbad, Forgetting Sarah Marshall,* and *Pineapple Express.* She would ask if I wanted to stop by when I wasn't working, and I probably spent a total of forty days sitting in a chair with her behind the monitor, soaking everything up like a sponge. She'll never understand what a gift that was to me as a director. During *Pineapple Express,* I learned the right camera angles to convincingly shoot a fight scene. When Jonah Hill's character flashes back to his childhood obsession with drawing dick pics in *Superbad,* I noted all the camera tricks they did to make it so the child actors and the dick pics were never in the same room at once! It sounds funny, but it was all this old-school trick-of-the-eye stuff that I just loved. All these things helped me grow as a filmmaker.

Shauna never asked for anything in return, except to tell me that her boyfriend Ed was a huge fan. "Do you have any new movies with you?" she would ask. Or "Can you sign this?" It got to a point that I would just show up with DVDs and glossies pre-signed to Ed and hope they hadn't broken up.

They kept me around in their little family. In *Pineapple Express*, I played Jessica, the wife of the drug dealer played by Danny McBride. It was one the first movies he did. In the film, he references his wife who is in jail, so before production even started we had to take a ton of photos together so they could be framed about his house in the scene. Danny and I went to Echo Park in L.A. with a photographer, and I basically spent a day making out with him. They even put a bridal gown on me to fake our wedding photo. But what Danny and I loved was physical comedy. I got on his back and did a piggyback ride, then he said, "Okay, your turn." I did it! And we shared ice cream in this very sloppy gross way and I loved every minute of it.

Later, I was about to shoot a DVD extra for the film, so I was in the makeup trailer reveling in the fact that some chick was curling my hair for me. James Franco was in the next chair, dressed like his complete pothead character but completely engrossed in his schoolbooks for his classes at UCLA. Shauna came running in, excited to see me. "Oh, my God, yes, you're here," she said. "Ed is stopping by for lunch."

"I'm excited to finally meet him," I said.

"No, he is going to freak out," Shauna said. "Can you come say hi and take a picture? You can say no."

"Bitch, please," I said. "Yes, I can come by to take a picture with this Ed I feel like I know but have never met."

"Okay, we'll surprise him."

About an hour later, Shauna comes over to get me.

"Ed's here," she says.

"Oh, great," I said. I followed her around the corner and—hold up!—how is it that more than two years have gone by and no one tells me that Shauna's Ed is *Ed freaking Norton*?

"Hi there," I said.

Ed was so incredibly shy and said in the nicest, most genuine voice, "It is so nice to meet you." He was so nice that I thought he was acting.

"Okay," I said to Shauna. "Is your Ed here, or did you just get Ed Norton to prank me?"

"No, no, this is my Ed," she said, giving him a hug. He is indeed. They got married and have two kids, and now that quintessential California chick lives in New York.

When I was in the news a lot this year, Seth Rogen and Judd Apatow came forward as sort of character witnesses for me in the media. "I've known Stormy Daniels a long time, and I'll be honest, she may have mentioned some of this stuff around ten years ago," Seth recounted to Ellen DeGeneres on her show in April. "At the time, when you asked a porn star who they've been sleeping with and the answer was Donald Trump, it was like the least surprising thing that she could have said."

But I am getting ahead of myself.

THREE

Okay, so did you just skip to this chapter? Quick recap for those just joining us: my life is a lot more interesting than an encounter with Donald Trump. But I get it. Still, of all the people who I had sex with, why couldn't the world obsess over one of the hot ones?

So, let's go back to July 13, 2006.

It was really hot for Lake Tahoe, even for July. I was sitting in the back of a golf cart at the Edgewood Tahoe Golf Course, seeking shade and relief from the prattling of Jessica Drake. She and I were still contract stars for Wicked Pictures. As you know, we had history. For those of you just joining us, she slept with my boyfriend Brad behind my back, and I wanted to murder her. Little things.

Wicked had recently had a PR guy come in who was talking big about getting into some things that normally weren't available to an adult company. One of those opportunities was sponsoring a hole at the American Century Celebrity Golf Championship at Lake Tahoe. It's like Vegas in the Sierras, and the American Century is the casino town's biggest event of the summer. It has a bachelor party weekend feel, except there's no sucker getting married. Wicked's founder, Steve Orenstein, brought me, Jessica, and another contract girl—a brunette, to keep us blondes from throttling each other. Steve was sitting in the front of the golf cart, which showed what an important trip this was for Wicked. I can count on one hand how many work events he went to.

Our job for the day was simple: Celebrities would come through, and we'd say hello and offer them water or a snack. They could take a photo if they wanted. The brunette was in the process of separating from her husband *and* fighting with her then boyfriend, so we had lots to talk about to pass the time. Meanwhile, Jessica went method, standing around wearing a golf glove as if she spent every weekend on the links. She was all over everyone coming through like some kind of golf geisha.

She really turned on the act when Donald Trump came through. She did everything but pull out a lace handkerchief from her bra and drop it, like, "Oh!" The rest of us got out of the cart to join them, and we rolled our eyes at Jessica so hard you'd think we were having a collective seizure. Trump was wearing a yellow polo that clung to his stomach where it tucked into his khakis. He had a red cap, a Trump crest as a placeholder for the MAGA slogan not one of us could see coming.

Back then, Trump was just a charismatic businessman and *Apprentice* reality star. Playing the part, he came over to shake our hands. "I'm Donald Trump," he said, acting like he was hosting the event. "Thank you for coming today."

Steve introduced himself as the owner of Wicked. "These are my girls," he said, introducing Jessica and the brunette as contract stars. "And this is Stormy Daniels, contract star and contract director."

Trump cocked his head to look at me. "Oh," he said. "You direct? That's very interesting." I noticed he was looking at my face and not my breasts.

"I enjoy it," I said, before Jessica cut in.

"Do you want me to escort you to your next hole, Mr. Trump?" Jessica said, already taking his arm to drag him off. He took a look back at me, and I could tell he was curious.

When the tournament was done for the day, Wicked had a booth set up in a gifting suite. It was a similar thing to the course, with celebrities coming through getting free stuff. The funny thing about becoming rich and famous is that that's when people start giving you everything for free. We were giving out Wicked-branded bags with DVDs, alongside all the other sponsors handing out sunglasses and golf clubs. So, we were popular. There were lots of people there, but I was most excited to see Anthony Anderson and especially Kevin Nealon. My dream job was to be a writer for *Saturday Night Live,* and Tina Fey and Amy Poehler were my best friends in my head.

Trump came through with a bodyguard and once again, Jessica was all over him. I hung back, but he zeroed in on me. "Ohh, it's the director," he said. "That's really fascinating." We took a photo, and I know everyone has made a big deal of that picture, but I have that same one with twenty other celebrities that day. Trump kept going and I didn't think anything of it.

And then his bodyguard came back. He was in his late forties, mostly bald except for a wisp of close-cropped light hair up top. "Mr. Trump wants to know if you can have dinner with him tonight," he said.

I wasn't sure what to say. Steve, my boss, overheard and stepped over. "Here's my card," Steve said.

The bodyguard took it, but he kept looking at me. "My name is Keith Schiller," he said, and he gave me his number before asking for mine. "I'll be in touch later if you are interested."

I wasn't. Back in my room, I called the guy I was casually dating, Mike Moz. He was working as a publicist at the time.

"You'll never guess what happened," I said.

"You killed Jessica and threw her in Lake Tahoe," Moz said, deadpan.

"No, but I want to. Donald Trump wants to have dinner with me."

That got Moz's attention. "Well, are you gonna go?"

"*No,*" I said. This wasn't for Mike's benefit. It really didn't even seem like an option.

"What's wrong with you?" he said. "You have to go." Moz was very career focused and was always telling me about the importance of relationships in business and how it's all about who you know. "It's a great opportunity for you. Just think of it as a once-in-a-lifetime thing."

"I'm supposed to have dinner with Steve and Jessica," I said. Steve was taking us out to eat, and then we were all going to a silent auction.

"You don't want to go to that."

"Well, I'll see if he calls," I said, "because I don't care if I do or not."

What's funny is that sex never once entered my mind. Call me naïve, but he was one of the few straight guys—hell, any guy—who didn't immediately stare at my tits. Plus, he seemed really struck by the fact that I was a director. And I certainly didn't think he was asking me there as an escort. I never thought in that frame of mind because I wasn't an escort. And the girls that did it hid it, because Wicked had a strong policy against escorting.

I was hoping there would be no call and I would just have the decision made for me. But then Keith called.

"Mr. Trump wants to know," he said, so polite, "if you are interested in dinner tonight."

"Okay," I said.

He said we'd meet where Trump was staying, the Harrah's Lake Tahoe Hotel and Casino. "Do you want me to send a car?"

"I'm okay," I said. I'd been stuck on the golf course and in the gifting suite. It would be nice to walk. I had only brought one dress for the trip, my favorite. It was a little gold dress, and I loved it because I looked good in it and it was comfy like a T-shirt, with no straps to dig in. I called Steve as I put on a pair of gold strappy heels.

"I'm not going to go to dinner with you guys tonight," I said.

"Oh, really," he said, with something lascivious in his voice. "Why is that?"

"I'm having dinner with Donald Trump."

"Okay," he said. I couldn't tell if he said it that way because it sounded absurd or if he anticipated something I didn't.

The sun was starting to set as I started the walk over to the Harrah's hotel. As I passed a tattoo parlor, I heard a voice yell from inside.

"Stormy?"

"What the . . . ," I said, reeling. Alana Evans, who is also an adult actress, came running out of the tattoo parlor. I didn't know her well, but she was my downstairs neighbor in L.A. It was weird for both of us to see each other out of context.

"Are you here for the golf tournament?" I asked.

"No," she said, brushing back her long blond hair. "I'm actually just babysitting Cindy right now." Cindy Crawford—the adult actress, not the supermodel—was inside getting a new tattoo on her back. She looked at my gold dress and asked in her flat California accent, "Where are you *going*?"

"I'm going to have dinner," I said, "with Donald Trump."

"Oh, sure you are."

Looking back on the conversation, I realize she 100 percent thought that I was meeting a client and that she had busted me. Having dinner with Donald Trump sounded that far-fetched.

"No, I really am," I said. "Wicked is at the celebrity golf tournament. I met him and he wants to have dinner."

"I bet he does."

"Come with me," I said.

"Well, I can't," Alana said, looking back at Cindy.

"Maybe if I call you, you can get out of it."

"Oh, yeah, have Mr. Trump call me."

She totally didn't believe me, I thought as I walked on into the sunset. Little Red Riding Hood in strappy gold heels.

I called Keith's number when I got to Harrah's, assuming Trump would come down to the lobby and then we would go to dinner wherever he had chosen.

"Come on up," said Keith. "It's the penthouse."

This wasn't a red flag. I had been around enough celebrities to know sometimes they liked to show off and pull out the whole butler-and-personal-chef routine. Maybe dinner would just be upstairs.

When the elevator opened on the top floor, the penthouse

was the only room on the floor. There was a huge marble foyer with a checkerboard pattern of black and white. Keith was there, guarding a giant set of double doors, with one slightly cracked.

"It's so nice to see you," he said. He waved a hand at the door for me to enter, and I paused.

"Go on in," he said.

I tentatively pushed open the doors, and I remember my heels clacking on the marble. Inside the doors was a smaller foyer with a heavy wood table with a beautiful flower arrangement. And no Donald Trump.

"Hellllllllooo?" I called out.

And Trump came swooping in, wearing black silk pajamas and slippers.

"Hi there," he said.

Look at this motherfucker, I thought. I was just so mad.

"Excuse me, I have the wrong room," I said, adding a southern edge of polite malice to my voice. "Sorry to interrupt, Mr. Hefner. I'm looking for Mr. Trump."

His jaw went slack, and his eyes bugged.

"What are you *doing*?" I yelled. "Go put some *fucking* clothes on."

Like some sort of cartoon, he whizzed out of the foyer. I continued on into the room, which looked like an apartment. There was a long sideboard table with wineglasses and a complete living room setup and dining room table. I threw my purse on the couch and sat down, resigned to waiting for this idiot to get dressed.

I think he was scared I was going to leave, because he was back almost instantly. It was like he went in the phone booth and leapt out in a full suit. It was a nice one, dark navy, which he'd paired with a tie.

"That's more appropriate," I said. I was still mad.

"Can I get you a drink?" he asked, reflexively walking over to the wineglasses.

"Oh, I don't drink," I said.

He paused. "And you're . . ." He stopped himself. I know he really wanted to say, "You're a porn star and you don't drink?"

"No," I said.

"At all?"

"No."

It was true, back then I had at most two glasses of champagne a year.

He looked at me with the same face he made when he found out I was a director. "That's interesting," he said. "I don't drink, either."

"Not at all?" I said, taking my turn to be surprised.

"I don't like the taste of alcohol," he said. "And I find people make poor financial decisions when they've been drinking."

"*I know!* That's one of the reasons I don't drink. I've been stripping since I was seventeen, and I can't tell you how many clubs I've been in where girls get drunk and lose their money. I was like, 'Not for me.' I totally get it."

He smiled. "Our businesses," he said, "are kind of a lot alike, but different."

"Yeah!" We laughed.

"Well, can I get you a water?"

"Sure."

We started talking, which meant he proceeded to go on and on without asking me anything about myself. It was one pretentious brag after another. I will spare you. I found myself getting more and more offended. My Louisiana roots were showing, and this was just socially inappropriate. When you've invited someone to meet, it can't be a one-sided conversation. I'm not his therapist, and this was not a job interview.

Plus, I was freaking hungry. I needed a bowl of pretzels, at least, if I was going to sit through this. *You said there'd be dinner,* I thought. His monologue went on for a good ten or fifteen minutes, which is an eternity when your stomach's growling and you're alone with a bore.

"Have you seen my magazine?"

Wow, he actually asked me a question. I shook my head no.

"It's not out yet, but I have an advance copy," he said. "Would you like to see it?"

It didn't matter, he was already up. He grabbed a satchel sitting on the side table and pulled out the magazine to flash it in front of me. I know it was some kind of money magazine with him on the cover, and a lot of people assume it was *Forbes* because of the timing, but I didn't even look at it.

"Really?" I snapped, looking up at him. "Does this work for you normally?"

He looked perplexed. Like I'd asked a dog an algebra problem. Reader, I was hangry—the volatile mix of hunger and anger.

"Are you so insecure that you have to brag about yourself," I continued, "or are you just a fucking asshole? Which is it?"

He was so stunned, he just stood there. I lowered my voice to growl, "Someone should take that magazine and spank you with it."

"You wouldn't," he said in a quiet voice.

I held out my hand, palm up. "Hand it over," I said. When he didn't immediately give the magazine to me, I snatched it from him and rolled it up. "Turn around and fucking drop 'em," I said.

It was a power moment, not at all sexual. It wasn't dirty play or even foreplay. It was me being pissed off and him being shocked and neither of us wanting to back down from a challenge. He went to take it back and I wouldn't let him.

"I'm serious!" I said. For a second, I almost lost my nerve. He was still "The Donald," and he was much older than me. I was twenty-seven, and this guy was more than twice my age—an elder who should be respected.

But he turned, lowering his pants just enough for me to give him a couple of swaps. I got up and tossed the magazine on the side table with every intention of leaving. Because where do you go from that moment?

This is what stopped me: he turned around and said, in a slow, appraising voice, "I like you." He fixed the belt of his pants and added, "You remind me of my daughter."

Now, I know everyone has made that sound sexual, and I feel so sorry for Ivanka because she's had to hear all these things. Yes, he said what he said, but it was not a creepy or sexual conversation. It was not some perverted, "You remind me of my daughter. She's so hot." No, it was, "You remind me of my daughter." And these were the exact words he added: "You're smart, you're beautiful. You're just like her. *You're a woman to be reckoned with.*"

"Thank you," I said. His whole demeanor had changed. His peacock plumage was now folded down and he became a more normal human being.

"Do you know about my daughter? Have you seen her?"

"Yes, she's very beautiful." Because she is. She's stunning. It was a compliment, not a come-on. He seemed to be off-script. He was genuinely shocked that he'd just had his ass whipped. So, this was now the third time that I had seen him shocked. Once when he found out I was a director, then when he found out I didn't drink, and now that I had spanked him. He was walking around the room, and I could tell a plan was forming in his head.

"Have you ever seen my TV show?" he asked.

Oh, God, I thought, *here we go again.* When I didn't answer, he asked, "Have you ever watched *The Apprentice*?"

"No," I said, quick and dismissive. I thought we'd gotten past both the pajama seduction and annoying bragging portions of the evening.

"Wait," he sputtered. "Well, you know what it is. It's a huge hit."

"Yeah, I get the gist," I said. I'm not really a TV person, but the show had become inescapable in the two years it had been on. Reality stars were starting to be in the tabloids I read when I got my nails done. People like Omarosa were suddenly "celebrities," and "You're fired" was the big catchphrase.

He stopped pacing to look right at me. "*You*," he said, "should be on that show."

"What?"

"You should be on *The Apprentice*," he said. "You'd be fabulous on it. Fabulous. You'd be huge."

He was using all the outsized, grand words we know him for now. But it wasn't for show. He was having a genuine moment. An epiphany.

"They'll never let me on," I said.

"Why?"

"Because I am a porn star and it's NBC," I said. "Never gonna happen."

His lip curled just slightly at the mere suggestion of the word "no." It gave me an idea about how I could fuck with The Donald.

I leaned in and said slowly, "Even you aren't that powerful."

"What do you mean?" he said. "It's my show."

"I don't care. Even you can't do that."

Look, in my mind, one of two things was gonna happen: either he does it and I'm on *The Apprentice,* or I get to say "I told you so" and I take a couple more feathers out of his tail. Both were very appealing to me. I'd take either.

"No, if you want to do it, I think it would be great," he said, laying out his case. "First of all, it would show the world that you're not a stereotypical porn star, and people would tune in for the surprise. It would be sensational. Sensational. Second, it would be great for both of us. Imagine the ratings it will bring."

My friends have asked me if I think he was just leading me on, but I honestly feel that it was a genuine conversation. I could see his wheels turning and watched him do the mental gymnastics of a cost-benefit analysis in his head. I would bring a built-in fan base in a valuable demographic, and me on TV would be shocking, but not in the way people think. I truly believe his initial thought about this was with his brain, not his dick.

"I understand." I shrugged. "But you can't do that."

"No, here's the thing," he said. "I have a wild card. Every season I can pick someone, if I so choose, that doesn't have to be . . ." He trailed off. To this day I don't know what the selection and vetting process was, but whatever it was, I would skip right through. "You can be my wild card next year, and I think it would be sensational. This will be great. This could be huge."

"Uh-huh," I said, noncommittal.

"I've gotta think on this," he said, sitting down on the couch next to me. "So, are you married?"

"No," I said. "I was, but I'm not now. But you're married. What would your wife think of you being here with me?"

"Oh, don't worry about that," he said. "It's not a big deal, and anyway, we have separate bedrooms." I took that to mean that he no longer saw me as someone to sleep with. By spanking him, I wondered if I had alpha-dogged my way out of his writing me off as a bimbo. As if to prove his intentions were now legit, he jumped up to grab a photo. "Have you seen my son?"

He showed me a photo of Melania holding little Barron, who was only four months old. It was adorable, and I could tell it made him genuinely proud.

He asked me about my family and I gave him the briefest of bios, but I was impressed that he was at least showing some give-and-take in conversation.

"I have to ask you a question," he said. "It's kind of offensive, so I apologize in advance if you're offended."

"Go 'head," I said.

"What's the situation on royalties in the adult business?"

I laughed. I was expecting a sex question of some sort. He added, "I'm familiar with TV, and I've been in lots of movies, and I get these checks."

"There's nothing," I said.

"You're kidding me."

"I wish I was," I said. He was honestly beside himself. It

started a series of questions about the ins and outs—that joke is never funny—of the adult business. Porn 101 at Trump University. But it was nice. We had moved past the foolishness with the pajamas, and we could respect each other's insight as two career-obsessed people who happen to be extremely successful at what we do.

He asked how much money I made per scene and I explained that I have a contract. "If you're freelance you can make thirty grand per month," I said, "and you can get more for different sex acts."

"What do you mean?" he asked.

"Well, you get paid more for anal," I said. "A bonus on the back end, so to speak."

"Why isn't everyone freelance?"

"That's for the girls who get in the business and want to make as much money as fast as possible. They have a two-year plan or whatever, and they want to make that thirty grand a month and pay for college, whatever."

"What's the problem with that?" he asked.

"They get shot out," I said. "There's a very short shelf life in the adult business if you do too many films. You make a lot of money really quickly, your star rises really quickly, and then it's gone. Getting a contract, you get a lot less money but you're in it for the long run."

"Well, how much money *do* you make?"

At the time I was making seven thousand dollars a month from Wicked, including my writing and directing fees.

"Well, that's—" he said, making a face. *"Why?"*

"I make one movie about every six to eight weeks. There are girls who make six movies a week while I'm doing ten movies a year. I won't get shot out, plus Wicked spends millions of dollars advertising me and creating my brand. I can go out and do dance bookings and say I am a Wicked contract star. But I own the name 'Stormy Daniels' and stormydaniels.com. If I leave Wicked, I leave with my name. Whereas this other girl makes a whole bunch of money the first year and then she's out."

"So, you *are* smart," he said, nodding.

"Okay, I have a question to ask you that may be offensive," I said.

"Ooh," he said. "What is it?" I think he thought I was going to ask him something dirty, too.

I pointed to his hair. "This," I said, taking a long beat. "What's going on with *this*?"

"I know," he said with a smile. "It's ridiculous. Come on. First of all, I have a mirror. Second of all, I have had every celebrity stylist—even Paul Mitchell himself—wanting to give me a make-over. I could have whatever. I could basically have a head transplant if I wanted, okay?"

"Okay, well, why don't you?"

"Everybody talks about it," he said with an air of in-on-the-joke smugness. "It's my thing. It's *my* trademark. Plus, if I let this person do it, it will just piss off all these other people. 'Well, why did you let him do it?' I know a lot of people who would kill to do it. The best. The best of the best."

"Easy, Samson."

It was another shot at him, but he seemed to enjoy it. I wasn't putting on an act—that's just my personality and what I do to people who I work with. The Donald was no different. Just a bigger fish to fry, which made me want to turn up the heat. And while I had calmed down, I was still angry that I had to prove he couldn't just order me up like room service. Where was this dinner he promised, anyway?

"What do you like to do for fun?"

Oh, you're learning, I thought, *like, how to have a normal conversation.* "I ride horses," I said. "I don't have a horse right now because I am too busy, but one day I hope to go back to riding."

"Oh, I am thinking of doing this show-jumping thing." He actually was, and he ended up hosting the Central Park Horse Show at Trump Rink in New York. I told him I don't do Grand Prix show jumping and started to explain three-day eventing competitions, but I took pity on him as I saw his interest fading.

"Well," I said, "what else do you do besides golf?"

His eyes lit up when he heard "golf," which I think was all he heard. He literally looked like he woke up.

"You golf?" he asked.

"No, my tits are too big to swing."

"Well, if you ever want to check out one of my courses, they have fabulous restaurants. The best food in the world. If you ever want to, call me and I will set it up for you." That got him talking—at length—about his plans to build "the greatest golf course the world has ever seen" in Scotland. He said he was having a hard time getting it started.

He was getting agitated talking about it, but there was nothing that made him seem as petulant and prone to tantrums as he has been as president. He was just run-of-the-mill insecure, which I find happens a lot with people with money that they didn't earn themselves. They harbor this inner self-esteem problem that they try to mask by overcompensating. That's him to a tee.

He asked me where I lived, so he could recommend a course, and I told him I was thinking about moving to Florida. "Oh!"

he said, perking up again. "I'm building a new condo tower there. Tampa Bay. I'll get you a good deal." Mind you, there has been some confusion about that in the press. People, even my gay dad Keith Munyan, got the impression that Trump was going to *give* me a condo. No, he was going to *sell* me one.

"If I bought a condo from you, at least that might prove we met," I said. "My friend Alana didn't believe me. I said I would call her . . ."

"Let's call her," he said.

I dialed her number and she answered after a few rings. "I'm here," I said. I mostly called her because she thought I was lying and I couldn't stand that. "Come hang out with us."

"I'm with Cindy," she said. "I'll call you back."

I clicked off and he looked at me expectantly. "How do you know her?" he asked.

"She's actually my neighbor in L.A. and I randomly bumped into her," I said. "She's in the business."

"Is she a big star like you?"

"She's not a contract girl," I said, and he nodded. I smiled—I had taught him some of the language of the adult business.

"Have you worked with her?"

"No, I haven't directed her," I said. "But I have directed her husband a couple of times."

His eyebrows shot up. "She's married? How does *that* work?"

"Well, when a mommy and a daddy love each other very much . . . ," I started, as if I were speaking to a child. Then I laughed. "It's like any industry. You date who you meet, and when you work all the time, you're going to naturally click with people. There's a separation. You can love your job and the work you create, and you can also love someone."

That was all rainbows, but it was starting to be a pride thing for me that Alana wasn't calling back. This girl didn't believe me. I just needed her to know I wasn't making up a story. So, I called again, and when I got her I said, "Are you gonna come?"

"Yeah, come!" Donald shouted.

"Who is that?" asked Alana.

"That's Mr. Trump," I said. "I told you. Do you want to talk to him?"

He grabbed the phone, "Come out with us," he said. "Come party. Come have a good time."

I started cracking up because there was no alcohol and definitely no drugs. I mean, this is the lamest party ever, if this is a party. If someone says "come party with us," it sounds like some *Hangover*-style orgy with cocaine on gilded Trump-branded mirrors. And that's probably what Alana pictured. He should have just said, "Come tell me about royalties in the adult industry, and I'll tell you about my golf club. We'll drink bottles of water and it will be fabulous."

So I can totally understand why she thought the scene wasn't for her. She totally ghosted, which she has admitted in the press.

When I looked at my phone, I realized I had been there for three hours. We had been talking so much that I had lost track of time, and all that water made me have to pee. Well, first *he* was talking so much, but I'd taught him to actually have a conversation and be respectful. If I can help just one selfish person . . .

"Can I use the restroom?" I asked.

"Yeah, the closest one is right there through the bedroom."

"Thank you," I said.

I walked toward the bedroom, which was clearly the one he

had been sleeping in. The bed wasn't messy, but it was lived in. I went through another set of double doors to enter this big, truly beautiful bathroom. There were marble counters with two sinks, a big shower over here, and another door to a toilet. I used the bathroom and as I washed my hands I saw his stuff was on the counter.

Now, I am a bit of a serial killer in that I like to keep trophies from people I meet. Nothing valuable, I just like to have a little talisman to commemorate meeting someone. There was this brief moment when I thought about stealing something, but I didn't. But I did notice his toiletry bag was open. I didn't touch it or dig through it, of course, but his nail clippers and tweezers were on top and they were gold. *This guy,* I thought. His products were out—Old Spice and Pert Plus. I laughed out loud.

"Well, that explains your hair," I said under my breath. There was something so right and so wrong about a purported billionaire using a two-in-one shampoo and conditioner. I touched up my makeup a little and put on some lip gloss. I figured it was time to make a push to actually get dinner.

I came out and he was dead ahead on the bed.

He was perched on the edge, like he had tried out different poses. A poor attempt at looking powerful. He had taken off the suit, and was down to his white briefs, a white V-neck, and socks.

I had the sense of a vacuum taking all of the air out of the room, and me deflating with it. I sighed inwardly, keenly aware of two thoughts in that one moment. There was the simple *Oh, fuck. Here we go.* But there was also a much more complex, sad feeling that none of what he said was true. He didn't respect me. Everything he said to me was bullshit.

And I was mad at myself. How did I miss this? I have been

stripping since I was seventeen. I can read a room. I never caught it. For someone who is now famous for "Grab 'em by the pussy," you'd think he would have grabbed me by the pussy hours earlier. But up until that moment, he wasn't vulgar or suggestive. I thought we had a great conversation and we'd gotten past the pajama thing by making him my bitch and proving my worth. And it all meant nothing.

I should have said, "Again?" Let him know this wasn't okay. But I was just, well, sad. Moz, the guy I was seeing, liked to drop these sayings on me that annoyed the fuck out of me. One of them was "Put yourself in a bad situation, bad things happen." Right or wrong, I could hear his little voice in my head saying that. And the other voice in my head said, "Fuckin' Alana." If she'd been here, one of us would have been out there with him. He wouldn't have been able to take his pants off.

So, here we go.

It was an out-of-body experience.

I was lying down on the bed with him on top of me, naked. I was just there, my head on the pillow. There was no foreplay and it was one position. Missionary. We kissed and his hard, darting tongue pushed in and out of my mouth. I thought, *He's even a terrible kisser.*

I lay there as he fumbled his dick into me. I was surprised he didn't even mention a condom. I didn't have one with me anyway, because I wasn't meeting him for sex. If I had been, I always brought my own, because I am allergic to latex. Back then I used Avantis.

He was a little verbal, but nothing dirty. "That's great," he said. "That's great. Oh, you're so beautiful." I certainly didn't do any kind of performance. I just kind of lay there. A lot of women have been there. He wasn't aggressive, and I know for damn sure I could have outrun him if I tried, but I didn't. I'm someone who doesn't stop thinking, so as he was on top of me I replayed the previous three hours to figure out how I could have avoided this.

The world is waiting to hear about his penis. I know, I know. The expectation is that I will say it's some kind of micropenis. The point-and-laugh moment. I am sorry to report that it is not freakishly small. It is smaller than average—below the true average, not the porn average. I didn't take out the measuring stick.

He needs to shave his balls, I thought. They were unusually hairy, hairier than the rest of him. He had some fur all over, but I remember thinking, *Hmmm, he's got a lot going on down there.* But his hair down there was better than what was on his head.

I hope I haven't ruined lunch for you.

His penis is distinctive in a certain way, and I sometimes think that's one of the reasons he initially didn't tweet at me like he does so many women. He knew I could pick his dick out of a lineup. He knows he has an unusual penis. It has a huge mushroom head. Like a toadstool.

I lay there, annoyed that I was getting fucked by a guy with Yeti pubes and a dick like the mushroom character in Mario Kart.

And then it was over. He came on me, not in me. I'd say the sex lasted two to three minutes. It may have been the least impressive sex I'd ever had, but clearly, he didn't share that opinion. He rolled over and said, "Oh, that was just great." He let out a big sigh and added, "We're so good together, honey bunch." That would be his name for me from then on.

He looked over at me, expectant. All I could muster was a "Yeah."

"I'd love to see you again," he said. "We need to get together again."

When I didn't answer, he said in this grossly vulnerable voice, "Would you see me again?"

"Oh, uh, yeah." I was already planning how to get out of there.

"How can I get ahold of you, honey bunch?" he asked. How many women have been in this situation? *You're a bore, you're the definition of bad sex, you call me this insipid name, I want to teleport out of here and be somewhere eating snacks with my girlfriends—but sure, let's do this again.*

I gave him my number and he wrote it down on the Harrah's notepad next to the bed. *Keith already has my number, you dipshit,* I thought. *But sure, here.*

I got up to find the dress that had been my favorite, and sat back down on the bed, hurriedly putting on my heels. "What are you doing tomorrow?" he asked. He said he would be at a nightclub that was in my hotel and asked me to meet him there and bring a signed copy of what I thought was the best movie I had directed. Back then it was *3 Wishes,* which had just come out that May. Maybe he sensed my lack of interest in him, because he quickly added, "We need to see each other soon because we have business to discuss. We have to talk about getting you on *The Apprentice.*"

That's how the *Apprentice* thing became bait. I didn't want to have sex with him ever again, but he had convinced me that being on the show was at least a possibility. And he used that.

Before we leave this scene, I would like to note that it wasn't until very recently that I learned that Karen McDougal says she was having an affair with Trump and had sex with him in Lake Tahoe that weekend. Karen McDougal is the former *Playboy* Playmate whom he met in June 2006. She later sold exclusive rights to her story to American Media, Inc., the publisher of the *National Enquirer,* which never ran an article about the affair. I am not disputing any part of Karen's story, but I have been asked if I saw any signs of another woman being at his hotel. I can only say there were no signs whatsoever that there had been a woman there. I don't know if he threw her shit in the closet or if he had a few rooms going, but I didn't smell a woman. There were no tampons, no makeup wipes, and I can tell you that I know Karen McDougal was not using Old Spice and Pert Plus.

I humored him and hung around for at most ten more minutes, but all of his questions about seeing me again made me claustrophobic. "When are you coming to New York?" he asked as I put my gold dress back on—the one that used to be my favorite. "I need to see you tomorrow," he said.

I promised he would, and I let myself out. Keith was no longer guarding the doors. I pushed the down button on the elevator, finally letting out the sigh I'd been holding in.

FOUR

You know that moment when you're watching a horror movie and the girl thinks she can go back into the house and get her cat or whatever? And you just shake your head because you know exactly where this is going?

Well, for me "the cat" was getting on *The Apprentice*. So, come along with me as we go back into the house.

I got a call from Keith Schiller the day after Trump and I met up. "Mr. Trump would like to see you tonight." He was going to be in the nightclub downstairs in my hotel. When I went down, Keith met me in the lobby.

"I'll take you to the table," he said. The club had a very Vegas vibe, with a lot of booths and a dance floor in the back. Keith led me through to the VIP area, which was very dark. There was a long couch, and Trump was sitting in a corner with Ben Roethlisberger. Shortly before his twenty-fourth birthday, "Big Ben" had become the youngest quarterback to win the Super Bowl, leading the Pittsburgh Steelers to the win in Detroit that February.

They were in mid-conversation, but Trump stopped and

smiled at me. He made a kissy face like an invitation, and I just nodded. I sat next to Ben, who introduced himself.

"I was in Detroit when you won the Super Bowl," I told him.

"Oh, you went to the game?" he asked. He leaned in to hear me over the DJ's cheesy pop.

"No, I was dancing," I said. "I was feature dancing at a place."

"Oh, where?" he asked, his face breaking into a wide smile.

"The Coliseum."

"Oh, I know that place," he said. "It's really nice."

Trump started talking to Ben and it seemed to be private, so I just looked around. Ben was drinking as Trump droned on. I don't drink, so I didn't have a cocktail to occupy me, and this was obviously before we all became phone zombies. My eyes wandered around the room, which seemed to be full of aging frat boys in town for the golf tournament. Keith was standing guard, and Ben had a guy, too. He was so much smaller than Ben that it seemed comical to me that this six-foot-five professional football player would need him.

I jumped in when there was a break in Trump's monologue. "Where's your ring?" I asked Ben. I meant his Super Bowl ring.

"Oh, when I go out I don't want to draw attention," he said, "so I have my guy hold my jewelry." I found it extra funny that this guy had all this jewelry belonging to Ben Roethlisberger in his pocket.

"Do you want to try it on?" Ben asked. He called his guy over, and two of my fingers fit in Ben's Super Bowl ring.

"It looks good on you," he said. "Do you come to Pittsburgh a lot?"

"Yeah, I'm actually going to be there in a couple of months dancing at a place called Blush."

"Oh, that place is kind of weird," he said. "You should take my number." I wondered what he considered "weird" and what he thought he was going to protect me from at a strip club. He gave me his number and I put it in my phone.

"Is this your real number or your ho phone?" I asked as I typed.

Trump and Ben both laughed, and Ben recited a second number.

"I'm not gonna call you on your ho phone," I said.

Trump grabbed Ben's shoulder and leaned in. "I told you she was smart," he said. "What did I tell you about this one?"

Yeah, what did he tell Ben about me? I wondered.

We were there an hour, tops, when Trump said he had some phone calls to make, some sort of business. He got up to leave and asked me again to let him know when I was in New York.

"Wouldn't she be great on the show?" Trump said to Ben, and then to me: "We need to talk about *The Apprentice*."

"That would be great," I said.

He paused and bent to talk closer to my ear. "Hey, I don't think it's a good idea for you to go upstairs unescorted," he said. He was right; it was late and people were drunk and things happen in hotels. "Also," he added, "I shouldn't really be seen with you." Which was also true, because we couldn't just walk through the lobby together and then go up in the elevator to my room. There wasn't even a hint that he was going for Round Two.

"Is it okay," he asked, "if I have Ben walk you to your room?"

I paused before answering. Why wouldn't he just have Keith walk me? He's literally a bodyguard.

"Do you mind?" he asked again.

As I have looked back at this in recent years—being older and wiser and less naïve—I still can't really figure out this situation. I don't want to imply it's something that it's not, but I also don't want to sound like an idiot.

"Okay, yeah," I said.

We stayed about fifteen more minutes, and Ben took me up the elevator to my floor, leaving his guy downstairs. Standing next to me, he seemed so much bigger than down in the bar—over a foot taller than me.

"Thank you," I said, getting out of the elevator.

He didn't say anything and just continued to walk with me. I looked up at him. His brow was tightly knit, and his eyes seemed predatory. As I went down the corridor with Ben, all of my intuition alarms went off. The voice that goes, *This guy's not getting a private dance. Don't go in a VIP room with this man. This is what I felt.*

At my door, Ben said, "Oh, can I see your room?"

"I'm really tired," I said, awkwardly holding the key card.

He looked at the card until I put it in, and I didn't open the door all the way. Just enough for me to slip through. As I got behind it, keeping my face out, I noticed he'd raised his hand to rest it on the door.

He pushed lightly, I pushed lightly. Did he know he was leaning on the door? Was he just steadying himself?

"Can I come in?" he said.

"I'm just so tired," I said.

"How about a good night kiss?"

"Well, no, I am here with your friend," I said, literally trying to play the Trump card. "I just feel weird because I am going to be doing some business with him."

I was terrified. I am rarely terrified.

"Come on," he said.

"Maybe I'll call you when I'm in Pittsburgh," I said. We were each using the same amount of force to keep the door exactly where it was.

Stop being polite, Stormy.

In one move, I suddenly increased the pressure enough to slam the door and throw the latch.

"Good night!" I said, keeping a smile in my voice.

He stood outside, not leaving. Every now and again he'd knock, rapping his knuckles in a line low along the door. *"Come onnnn,"* he repeated in a singsong voice. "I won't tell." He stayed a few more minutes.

Let's be completely up front. If he wanted to get in that room, he could have the second I put the key card in the slot. If he didn't want the door to close, he could have put his foot right on the threshold. I am only describing my intuition.

I can't know what Trump intended when he sent me upstairs with Ben. I kept thinking of what Trump said: "What did I tell you about this one?" Had he told him, "Hey, she's down?"

I have no way of knowing, and I don't want to speculate.

I went back to L.A. the next day and life went on. Alana called to apologize for ghosting, and I said something vague about Trump wanting to have sex, but I didn't elaborate. I said something similar to Moz, leaving out the fact that we'd actually had sex. I didn't tell anyone, and gradually the night with Trump at Harrah's just became another anecdote. I had always wanted to write a book like Chelsea Handler, and mine would be called *Why Me?* This would just have been a goofball chapterlet about

"My Night with The Donald." He gave me a number to reach him through his secretary Rhona Graff. I never called him.

But he kept calling *me*. The number always came up as UN-KNOWN, but he was the only one who bothered to have an anonymous caller ID, so I always knew it was him. He had an uncanny knack for calling while I was in the studio doing a photo shoot with Keith. Or I would be on set, directing a film, and I would say to everyone there, "Donald Trump is calling me." He didn't call weekly, but on an average of every ten days. I would put him on speaker, which he knew, and he would say, "Honey bunch! How's your day?" I did this at least a dozen times, his distinctive voice filling the room. None of these people knew I'd actually had sex with Trump, and I also didn't let anyone know about his plan to put me on *The Apprentice*. I was convinced that Jessica Drake would snake her way into my spot if she knew it was even a possibility. I actually sent him to voice mail quite a bit, because I didn't feel like dealing with him when I was busy.

"Honey bunch, I just saw you on a magazine cover," he would usually say. "It's fabulous. I was walking by and saw you." He used this as an excuse to call me. "I thought to myself, *That's my honey bunch. She looks fabulous, I have to call and let her know*. I can't wait to see you."

He let me know, constantly, that he was working on getting me my spot on *The Apprentice*. And he had an idea.

"I've been thinking about your *Apprentice* thing," he told me during one of his calls, and he then proceeded to lay out a plan that he would bring up again and again in our phone conversations and in-person meet-ups. "Here's the thing, honey bunch," he said. "We can't just get you on the show. If you get on the show and then you lose the first episode, that's actually worse than you not getting on at all."

"Yeah, of course," I said. Going home right away would just solidify the notion that I'm a dumb porn star who couldn't hang. The show was built around contestants split into two teams, called "corporations," challenged with a new business-related task in each episode. Each episode ended with Trump judging the performance of members of the losing team and eliminating the weakest link in the challenge with "You're fired!"

"Every episode you're on is better for ratings for me and more money for you," he said, before taking a long pause. "Gotta figure out a way to keep you on . . ."

"What do you mean?"

"We'll figure out a way to get you the challenges beforehand," he said. "And we can devise your technique."

He was going to have me cheat, and it was 100 percent his idea. He was going to tell me what the tasks were ahead of time, then devise a strategy to win. He never said he would rig it so I would win the whole thing, but he wanted to supply me with an unfair advantage. I felt very uncomfortable with it.

For six months, we talked on the phone and the plan came up repeatedly. He never once used the word "cheat"—he would talk about strategy and technique. "We have to make sure you stay on, honey bunch."

I didn't see Trump in person again until the next year. He invited me to the January 17, 2007, launch of Trump Vodka. The party was at Les Deux in Hollywood, and the crowd was a gaggle of wannabe stars, including Kim Kardashian, who was two months away from the release of the sex tape that would make her a star. I had just been in Las Vegas to accept the Contract Star of the Year honors at the AVN awards.

I was smarter now, so when he invited me, I brought along my friend Tera Patrick, who is also an actress in adult film. I wore dark jeans and a gold embroidered top. After we did the red carpet, Trump waved me over as soon as I walked in and kissed me on the mouth in front of everyone.

"You made it, honey bunch!" he said, his hand on my waist. He was wearing a pale platinum tie and a navy suit. I looked around for any sign of Melania, but she wasn't there.

"I did!" I said. I introduced him to Tera, and he brought me over to meet his son Don Jr. Don was there with his then-wife Vanessa, who was pregnant with their first child. I know from recent reports that Karen McDougal was at the party. He didn't introduce us, but as I go back in my memory I think I remember her in the VIP area. My hat's off to him for having the balls to juggle two women at the party.

Trump told me he was staying at the Beverly Hills Hotel and asked if I would come to his hotel later that night.

"Oh, I can't," I said. "I'm flying out of LAX tonight." It was actually true. I was heading to a dance booking.

"When can I see you again?" he asked. "When are you coming to New York?"

"I'll actually be there in a couple months," I said. I had a dance booking set for the week of my birthday in March.

"Well, call my office," he said. "I want to make sure I see you. And we can discuss our project."

There was the *Apprentice* bait again, and I took it.

I called Trump's secretary Rhona when I was in New York and she said to be there at twelve thirty that day. I didn't want to go alone, so I brought this girl Yoli, who was working for me as an assistant. We went right up to his office on the twenty-sixth floor of Trump Tower. He met us, so excited to show us all the memorabilia in his office, which seemed cluttered.

"I wish it was not so dreary today," he said, "because the view is *fabulous*."

"I'm still working on your thing, darling," he said quickly as I looked out on the fog blanketing Central Park. "Where are you dancing? It's so nice to see you."

I was dancing at a club called Gallagher's 2000 in Long Island City, but he barely let me get half of that out before he started talking again. I stopped him short by making fun of his eyebrows.

"You gotta trim that stuff," I said, maybe showing off for Yoli but mostly just keeping him in check. "They're out of control. You look like a Muppet."

"I'm so busy," he said, laughing. "I'm dealing with all this beauty pageant stuff."

Yoli perked up. She loved pageants, and honestly, it was hard to get her excited about anything.

"Do you want to go to the pageant?" he asked me.

"*Yes!*" Yoli screamed before I could say anything.

Fuck, I thought.

"Oh, I'll get you the best seats," he said. "It's in Hollywood. It will be fabulous. Fabulous."

The Miss USA pageant was the following week, on March 23. Trump sent a limo to pick up me and Yoli, who was practically vibrating with excitement. It was at the Kodak Theater in L.A., which was at least nice for me because that's where they host the Academy Awards.

I went to the Will Call. "There should be two tickets for Stormy Daniels."

"Okaaay," said the woman. "Who set them aside for you?"

"Uh, Mr. Trump?"

She seemed surprised, and I had a momentary panic that we had gotten Yoli's hopes up for nothing. Maybe he was afraid to use his name?

"Here we go," said the woman. "These are great seats."

She was right. They were about five rows back, behind press and family. Yoli was *riveted*, but I don't remember any of it. I saw Trump onstage, but I didn't interact with him at all. He called me after so I could assure him it was great.

The pageant host, Nancy O'Dell, was pregnant, and we would all later find out that Trump had used that as an excuse to try to fire her. Nancy was the "Nancy" Trump was talking about turning him down on the 2005 *Access Hollywood* "grab 'em by the pussy" tape released by *The Washington Post* in October 2016. "I did try and fuck her. She was married. And I moved on her very heavily. . . . I moved on her like a bitch, but I couldn't get there. And she was married. Then all of a sudden, I see her, she's now got the big phony tits and everything."

Hey, watch how you talk about big phony tits, asshole.

And then Shark Week happened.

The evening of July 29, 2007, Moz drove me to meet Trump at the Beverly Hills Hotel on Sunset Boulevard. By then, Moz and I were more serious, and I still had never told him that I had had sex with Trump.

As we drove up the driveway lined with palm trees, I went over my escape plan with Moz. "If I text you, call me and say it's an emergency."

"He's not going to kill you, Stormy," he said.

"*In case* he makes a move, you've gotta get me out of there."

Keith Schiller met me outside the hotel and led me to one of the private bungalows in the back of the hotel. The cottages, with pastel pink and green exteriors, were tucked in among acres of citrus trees and flowers that were absolutely beautiful. Keith let me into Trump's bungalow, where he was waiting.

"Honey bunch," he said, "you made it. I'm ordering us dinner. You must have the steak. It is fabulous. Fabulous."

I was just relieved that we were actually going to have food this time.

"We're almost a done deal getting you on the show," he said. This season they were doing it with celebrities, which he assured me I was. "You're a star, darling," he said.

"Well, that would be great," I said. "I would love to be on the show." Why the hell else was I hanging out with him? Clearly, I wanted to be on the show.

"We gotta figure out the challenges," he said. "The season hasn't started yet, so I don't know what we're gonna do. But we'll figure it out." He started going on and on about how much he hated Rosie O'Donnell, which seemed like such an insane tangent. Like, let's get back to me getting on the show. I later found out he had offered her a huge amount of money to compete on *Celebrity Apprentice* and she turned him down.

When the food came, I made him cut my steak. Not because

I am a kid, but because I just have a thing about meat on the bone. He thought it was funny and went out of his way to apologize for not knowing. Near the end of dinner, he checked the time and hurried over to the couch.

"It's Shark Week," he said. He turned on the Discovery Channel and stretched his arm on the edge of the couch. "Come here, honey bunch," he said. I inwardly groaned, but sure, let's cuddle and talk about me getting on your show. I sat under the crook of his arm as he became entranced by the documentary *Ocean of Fear: The Worst Shark Attack Ever.*

"Have you heard about this?" he said. "It's horrible. Horrible."

I hadn't, not being quite as up on sharks as I would learn he was. It's the incredibly dark and tragic reenactment of the aftermath of the World War II ship *Indianapolis* sinking in July 1945. They were adrift in shark-infested waters, and the sharks were swarming because of the blood in the water from the dead and injured. Most of the sailors didn't die in the actual sinking, but then the sharks just picked them off. Six hundred people.

So, I was sitting in this beautiful bungalow, and I was watching this crazy documentary filmed with real sharks tearing at bodies. And to say this guy was riveted is an understatement. I tried bringing up the *Apprentice* thing between shark bites, but he kept putting me off. "Disgusting creatures," he said. "Disgusting."

Then, to make it crazier, Hillary Clinton called. I could hear her voice through the receiver, and that accent saying "Donald."

"Hello, Hillary," he said, briefly distracted from the sharks. He kept the movie going but started pacing around the room.

She was up against Barack Obama seeking the Democratic

nomination, and he had a whole conversation about the race, repeatedly mentioning "our plan." They also discussed a family trip they wanted to take together—something involving a ski area. Who knows if Hillary was just humoring him.

Even while he was on the phone with Hillary, his attention kept going back to the sharks. At one point he covered the phone to talk to me.

"I hate sharks," he said. "I'll donate to just about anything, but the only shark charity I would donate to is one that promised to kill all the sharks."

I nodded, but thought, *Well, that's stupid, because they are part of the food chain. Obviously, they serve a purpose.*

When he hung up, he was effusive about Hillary. "I love her," he said. "She is so smart." This would be the fourth time he had donated money to her political career. Trump told me he and Hillary were great friends and that they had gone to the weddings of each other's children. Not quite true. The Clintons attended his wedding to Melania, but maybe he didn't want to bring her up.

"A lot of people say I should run for president someday," he said in passing, as he made his way to the couch. "They want me to run because I can afford it. Who would want to? This is way more fun."

Finally, after two hours of carnage, the sharks were done eating. And Donald was ready to make his move. He turned to look at my face appraisingly.

"What?" I said.

"Your nose looks like a little beak, darling."

"That's not a compliment," I said, kind of mad.

"No, like an eagle's."

"Also not a compliment!" I yelled.

"No, no," he said, "it's regal."

"You really aren't very good at this," I said.

Then he started to trace his finger on my thigh.

"Oh, I can't. I'm on my period." Which wasn't true.

Those were the magic words, though, and he was now totally not interested in pursuing sex that night. After all, you can't have blood in the water.

The next time we talked, he called me to tell me that I had been right. There was no spot for a porn star on *Celebrity Apprentice.*

Okay, we're done here, I thought.

"I told you that even you couldn't do it," I said, twisting the knife.

"Well, it was a personal favor to one of the executives," he told me. His wife had such a huge problem with a porn star contestant that she threatened to leave the guy, he said. "This bitch Roma."

"Rhona?" I said. What did his secretary have to do with this?

"Roma," he said. I can only assume he meant *Touched by an Angel* star Roma Downey, the wife of *Apprentice* executive producer Mark Burnett.

"I'm sorry, darling," he said, "It's not because I couldn't use my wild card. It's because *she* was gonna have a huge problem." He called her a bitch.

At this point, Moz and I were engaged, and this whole thing with Trump had become so tiresome. "Okay," I said.

He called once or twice more after that, but I didn't answer.

There was one final phone call, early on the morning of January 4, 2008. I was renting Keith's place in Valley Village in L.A. at the time, and Trump called from New York, oblivious to the time difference. I answered with an incredibly angry voice because it was so early.

It terrified him. He was sputtering about me being mad about something and I could just make out him saying "Jenna Jameson." I guess Tito Ortiz was a contestant and his girlfriend, Jenna, got some screen time on the show the night before. He was freaking out that I would be furious that the show had let another porn star on when he couldn't get me on.

"She's not very smart," he said.

"I didn't see it, I don't really care."

"You didn't watch the show?" he asked.

"No."

"Really?"

"Really," I said. "Okay, I gotta go."

"Good-bye, honey b—"

I clicked the phone off. *Well, that's done,* I thought.

Life goes on. It's easy to move on from bad sex with a billionaire and his fizzled plan to game out his reality show competition.

I didn't think about Trump again unless I was flipping through channels and saw him on my way to a more interesting show. *I had sex with* that, I'd say to myself. *Eech.*

FIVE

It was a Saturday morning, and I was already in heels and a sexy cop costume, chasing Adam Levine through the sketchiest part of downtown L.A. This was July 7, 2007, a few weeks before Shark Week. I was hired to appear in the Maroon 5 video for "Wake Up Call," the second single off their second album. Jonas Åkerlund was directing it as a trailer for a fake NC-17 film starring Adam as a guy covering up a murder. Jonas had already directed videos for Madonna, the Rolling Stones, U2, and Metallica, so it was pretty awesome to be on the set.

"Can I get a gun?" I asked the props guy.

"No," he said.

"How about a Taser?" I said.

"Nope," he said.

Thunder and Lightning would have to be intimidating enough. It was such a big video, complete with a car exploding, that the head of the label, James Diener, came to the set. A little under six feet tall, with a shaved head, James is a New Yorker and natural-born talent scout.

"Hey, you direct, right?" he asked me during a down moment.

"Yes," I said.

"I have this really cool idea," he said. "I have this new band I just signed, completely different vibe than Maroon 5. They're still working on the album, but it would be pretty sensational if you directed their video."

At that point, directing a music video was on my wish list. I had been watching everything Jonas did on set. This seemed like my way into that world.

"What's the name of the band?" I asked.

"Hollywood Undead."

A couple of weeks later, James emailed me the unmastered version of what would be the band's debut album, *Swan Songs*. "I think the first single is going to be 'Undead,'" he wrote. I played it, ready to start thinking of visuals. And I hated it. There was no way I was going to direct this as my first video. Fortunately, the album kept getting pushed back, all the way to September 2008, and then the date they chose to shoot the video changed to a time when I would be directing a film. By then I had married Mike Moz and realized that I needed to figure a way out of that because it just wasn't working. He had been a great motivator in business but was a nonstarter as a husband. I know what you're thinking: Didn't she learn from the first marriage? Believe me, I asked myself that same question. The problem was that he was so enmeshed in my business that it would take some time for me to get out.

"I have a lot on my plate right now," I told James.

"Well, could you be one of the girls in the video?" James asked me. They needed someone to make out with the lead singer.

"Sorry, no," I said.

The finished album was a hit, especially with tweens. It's rap rock, with the band members all having pseudonyms like J-Dog and wearing spooky masks. It wasn't my style, but I just kept hearing about them, whether it was a girlfriend saying she was auditioning for one of their videos or dating one of the guys from the band. It became a running joke, and I'd roll my eyes every time I heard the band mentioned yet another time.

I was living in Tampa and I had a friend there named Kayvon Sarfehjooy, a DJ and producer. On April 9, 2009, he called me to tell me his friend's band was playing 98Rockfest the following night at the St. Pete Times Forum, now called the Amalie Arena.

"They get in tonight, and you should come out," she said. "They're scene kids from Hollywood. You could direct their video."

That got my interest. By then I had directed the "Ballad of Billy Rose" video for a band called 16 Second Stare. "What's their name?"

"Hollywood Undead," he said.

"What the fuck?"

"It's a cool name," he said.

"The universe just keeps trying to make this happen," I said.

"Make what happen?"

"Fuck if I know," I said.

Kayvon thought I would hit it off with Jorel Decker, the aforementioned J-Dog, but it was also a chemistry test with the band. Now that they were popular, I was interested in directing their next video. We met up at a club across the street from the arena. It was a small place, but not so small that it could hide that it was dead on a Thursday night. It was a Tampa club trying to look Miami, with clean lines and white lacquer. We got a table and the band got me a bottle of champagne. I wore a white dress, so I looked like I was doing some sort of camouflage with the white tables and couches. I could see what Kayvon meant about them being sceney. They were dressed nice for supposedly hard rockers.

Girls started arriving, and they were all over the band. I wasn't looking to hook up with anyone—I was still looking to get rid of Moz—so that was the end of my conversation with Jorel. He got up and was talking to a blonde. So, I sat on the couch, the only one left sitting at the table because all the guys got up to hit on the women. I texted for reinforcements, and a girlfriend, Amanda, said she would come. In the meantime, I would just people-watch—take in the mating dance of rockers and hot girls.

Two guys walked in and went straight to the bar for drinks. Neither was dressed up, and one guy especially looked like a bum. He had a white Iron Maiden T-shirt with the sleeves cut off, shorts, and Vans slip-ons. After he'd downed a tequila, I caught him turning to look at me quickly before turning back to the bartender. He had two more shots, then wandered over to where I was sitting alone on the couch. He looked even filthier up close, but handsome. He had long brown hair, tattoos all up and down his arms, and gauges in his ears, which I'd never seen before. A rocker guy with a soccer player body.

"Hey," he said. "How's it going?"

"Fine," I said, my tone in keeping with the international code for "Not interested."

"Can I buy you a drink?"

I reached for the champagne and held it up as answer.

"Oh, yeah," he said.

He came around the table to sit right next to me and then asked, "Is anybody sitting here?"

I turned to look at both ends of the long empty couch. "Nope."

"Hi, I'm Glen," he said.

"Stormy."

"I'm the drummer for Hollywood Undead," he said.

"That's cool."

"So, what do you do?"

"Oh, that's cute," I said. "We're gonna play that game." I was so pompous about it, but in my defense, I knew that the band knew they were coming to meet Stormy Daniels about directing the video. But in his defense, he was the drummer. And bands don't tell the drummer anything. I realized he had no idea who I was, so I felt bad. I told him about my work with Wicked and he was completely unfazed. "Oh, that's cool," he said.

My friend Amanda arrived, and as she walked over I could see her taking note of all the slick band members—and the homeless guy next to me. She cocked her head, as if to say, "Um, excuse me, what are you doing?"

"This is Glen," I said. "Drummer."

She nodded, not offering her name. Suddenly Kayvon came over. "Hey, they want to get out of here," he said.

"Um, no surprise," I said. "There's nobody here."

"Do you think you can get us into the Penthouse Club?"

"You walk in the door and there's an eight-foot poster of me, so it would be pretty embarrassing if I couldn't," I said. I was on the February 2007 *Penthouse* cover. Plus, I knew the owner. "Let's go," I said, already switching into hosting mode.

In the parking lot, the guys all paired off with the girls and everyone was climbing in cars. Except Glen, who looked like a lost puppy. He had cabbed it over and didn't fit in anybody's car. I was getting into Amanda's car, which was a really beautiful white Mercedes.

"Do you need a ride?" I called to Glen.

As he turned, Amanda hissed at me. "He is not getting in my car," she said through a closed smile.

"Come on," I said.

"Dude," she whispered to me. "I just had it detailed."

"He's harmless," I said.

"Dirty," she said.

"Here, Drummer Boy," I yelled to Glen, overruling her. "Get in."

The Penthouse Club is a study in neon and black, bright pinks and blues highlighting the bodies of the best strippers in town. When I turn into host, I'm like a cross between a cruise director and a dominatrix. You will have fun on my watch. I was talking to all the guys because I was trying to get the directing gig, but something kept bringing me back to Glen. He was constantly needing to find a place where he could smoke, so I would lead him places. If he wanted me alone, he had more game than I gave him credit for.

"You looked like an angel at that club," he said, exhaling smoke up and away from my face. I laughed.

"No, serious," he continued. "I turned around and saw you all in white on this white couch. There was a spotlight on you and I thought, *I gotta go talk to that girl.*"

He was dirty because he'd missed his first flight and had come straight from band practice. He said he'd done the tequila shots to get the nerve to say hi. He didn't even like tequila and was more of a vodka guy. He'd been in bands right out of high school, living on the road with one band after another. We were both refugees of the road, and I began to feel that familiar feeling of wanting to look after someone. It creeps on me and I just think, *Oh, shit.*

"What's your favorite band?" he asked.

"You wouldn't know them."

"I'm a musician," he said. "I like all kinds of music. What, is it country?"

"No."

"Try me," he said, taking a drag on his cigarette. "And you better not say Hollywood Undead."

"Trust me, Drummer Boy, no," I said, moving closer to Glen to make way for a couple of guys taking their drunk friend home.

"Why are you so sure I've never heard of them?"

"Because they're a local band from Baton Rouge, where I'm from," I said. "They broke up while I was in high school."

"Why did they break up?" Glen asked.

"The bass player got killed and they never got a new one."

He got a look on his face that I couldn't quite read. "What if I do know what this band is?"

"If you know this band," I said, "we are totally going to get married and have a baby one day."

"Now you *have* to try me."

"Acid Bath."

He started singing, low, a smile creeping onto his face. "A creature made of sunshine, her eyes were like the sky . . ." he sang. It was one of my favorite Acid Bath songs, "Scream of the Butterfly."

"Great," I said, "now I'm stuck with you."

We went back inside, just before the Penthouse Club stopped serving alcohol. The other guys in the band started to leave, but I didn't want the night to end. I suggested that the next county over served alcohol later, and basically browbeat Amanda into driving us to the bar at the Hard Rock Casino.

We sat at the bar until four or five in the morning, with Amanda our over-it chaperone. She was miserable, cradling her head in her hands and absently eating peanuts left on the bar. Every bit of her body language said, *Can we go now?*

No.

"Are you coming to the show tomorrow?" he asked.

"No."

"That's a bummer," he said.

"Yeah, real bummer," said Amanda. "Listen, it's five o'clock. I'm gonna go pee, and then I'm leaving with you or without you."

As she trudged off, Glen leaned in toward me. "We should exchange numbers and keep in touch," he said.

"It's a waste of time," I said. "It's never gonna happen."

"Why not?"

"You and I live the same life," I said. "We're each like that thousand-to-one person that people meet, but every person is a thousand to us because we meet so many people. We say, 'Oh, keep in touch' every single night and we never mean it. Everyone gives us a card, we give our number, but we never have any intention of answering the text or ever talking again."

"But what if I promised to call you?"

"Okay, Drummer Boy," I said. "No. Our lives are just too complicated."

We left, and Amanda dropped me off first. I slipped away,

doing a Cinderella rush out of the car with a quick wave. Good-bye, Drummer Boy.

And I was fine with that, until I was sitting in a nail salon the next day. As the nail tech did my nails, I was seized with this one thought: *I have to see that guy again.* I had this impulse to jump up and run to find him, like some crazy heroine in a movie, but I didn't even know this guy's last name. My adrenaline was surging, and it felt like the universe had given me a chance at something after giving me all those hints about Hollywood Undead. I had fucked up. And when you screw up and need help, you call a lawyer.

My entertainment attorney was a guy named Mark, who I knew represented Disturbed, a band that would also be at that night's 98Rock show.

I'm sure I sounded like I was a hostage. "Mark, I need to get into the Disturbed show."

"Done," he said. "I'll take you." He drove in from the opposite coast of Florida and got us tickets and wristbands. Once I got in, it was like *Not Without My Drummer.* I just started asking everybody if they knew Glen, not knowing that he didn't go by Glen in the band. Anyone affiliated with Hollywood Undead, with their silly nicknames, all just knew him as Biscuitz. Finally, they came onstage to play.

They were even worse than I remembered.

It was early, so the place wasn't packed. I was near the front, so he spotted me. He pointed a drumstick at me and smiled. The music wasn't for me, but he is such a gifted drummer. It shone through to me. As soon as they were done, he came and grabbed me.

"Drummer Boy!" I yelled.

"Come backstage," he said. "I need to finish breaking down my kit."

"I can't go back there," I said. "I don't have a laminate."

He handed me his laminate, which was on his key chain. "Don't lose this, it has my house keys," he said.

"Did we just move in together?" I joked.

My attorney, having safely secured the drummer, was busy seeing to some of his clients. Glen and I hung out backstage, eating catering. It was like being back with Pantera. Running away with the circus. Vinnie and Rex from Pantera, Slayer's Kerry King, and, of course, Wookie . . .

"*Now* can I have your number?" Glen asked me. "Because I could have gotten you your own laminate, you know."

So we exchanged numbers. He didn't have his phone, so I wrote it on a slip of paper and put it in his pocket. Hollywood Undead needed to get on the bus for the next show. "Why don't you just wait on the bus with me until we leave," he asked. "I promise I won't kidnap you."

I agreed, and he stepped aside to let me get on the bus first. As I climbed in, I heard it.

"Stormy?"

I looked up, and there he was. Wookie. Of all the tour managers in the world, it had to be one I'd fucked on a tour stop at the Ritz.

"Oh, God," I said. "Hi, Wookie."

"How long has it been?" he asked, giving me a hug.

"Eight years," I said. Glen came in behind me, and Wookie gave him a nod of respect. Glen and I sat for a few minutes more in the lounge in the front, and then it was time to roll out. I handed him back his laminate.

"Here's your house keys," I said.

"I'll call you," he said.

He didn't. And I certainly wasn't going to call *him*. I'm a fucking lady, thank you. Two weeks went by, and I was in New York City for a dance booking. Moz and I were definitely separated now, and I was happy to be anywhere but Tampa, where I was letting him continue to live while he found work and got back on his feet. My roadie, Dwayne, couldn't work on the last night of the New York gig, so I was all alone in my hotel after the gig. It was about three in the morning, and I was eating Chinese takeout of sweet and sour chicken in my shitty hotel room.

I was lonely, and I looked at my phone. "Who would be awake right now?" I asked the empty room.

"Musicians," I answered myself.

All performers, whether they're dancers or musicians, are wired after a gig. On tour, Bus Call, the time you absolutely have to be on the bus every night, is usually between midnight and 3 A.M. Tour managers post a big piece of paper backstage listing the times for loading, catering info, what time you go onstage. And the very last thing is always the Bus Call in bold. That time is sacred, because they will leave without you.

When you get on the bus, you're spent but still wide awake. You're too wired still from being onstage in front of all those people and taking in all their energy.

So I just fired off a text before I could overthink it. "How's my Drummer Boy doing?" I literally dropped my phone, like it was on fire, not sure if I had just made a fool of myself. It buzzed with a text.

"Please tell me this is Stormy," said the message.

"Yes," I typed back, grinning.

Glen called immediately. He had written my number down and the last four digits had gotten blurred. He was on tour, and he told me he had been desperate to get in touch with me. We talked for the rest of the night and only stopped when I saw the sun begin to rise over Manhattan.

Any good old-time romance story has a moment where the hero gets drafted, right? Well, here goes.

In early February, one of my friends back home in Baton Rouge had sent me an email with the all-caps subject: HAVE YOU SEEN THIS?! It was a link to DraftStormy.com, a political movement asking me to run to represent Louisiana in the United States Senate. To convey my political bona fides, the site bragged that "at the age of seventeen, she was made editor of her high school newspaper, in addition to serving as president of her school's 4-H club, a service-oriented organization sponsored by the United States Department of Agriculture."

I was furious. I mean, the 4-H club thing was real and I'm damn proud of it, but someone was using my name and my image to further their political agenda without my permission. I am not political, and it's funny that most people don't even know that I'm a Republican. I tracked down the guy who started the campaign, Brian Welsh, and called him to tear into him. There was a lot of cussing, but it amounted to "I own the trademark to 'Stormy Daniels' and 'Stormy' in relation to things involving me and I am going to sue you to hell."

Brian let me go on for a long time, then finally said, "You're absolutely right. I'm sorry I handled this wrong. I didn't mean to insult or offend you. Let me explain myself."

"Five minutes," I said.

"Have you been keeping up with Louisiana politics?"

I was embarrassed that I had to say no. I'd been living in Florida and mainly on the road when I wasn't filming in L.A.

"Well, do you know who David Vitter is?" he asked. Republican senator David Vitter, a married dad of four, had successfully run on a staunchly antigay, antichoice, "family values" platform in 2005, only to have his name turn up on the list of Washington, D.C., madam Deborah Jeane Palfrey. There were unconfirmed rumors from *Hustler*'s Larry Flynt that Vitter's kink involved a diaper fetish. He apologized for his "sin," and I'm not judging that, but it made him a hypocrite. I hate hypocrites.

"Okay, I'm in," I said. "I'll think about it."

Brian flew me to New Orleans to meet him and introduced me to his team of political science geeks. He was in his late thirties, with brown hair and a Southern drawl. We talked, and even as his team filled me in on issues, I was adamant that I didn't want to run.

"Yeah, but this is great PR for you," said Brian.

"I'm not doing it for the PR, either," I said. "I don't want to make a mockery of the election process and political life." But I figured that if I could use my name to highlight topics like Planned Parenthood and sex education—which I am very passionate about—and expose this guy as a hypocrite who was not good for the average Louisiana resident, then I would. The

Stormy Daniels Senate Exploratory Committee was up and running, and we even had a campaign slogan: "Stormy Daniels: Screwing People Honestly." My endgame, and I said as much on national interviews with the likes of CNN, was to inspire someone more qualified to step up to the plate.

I started a listening tour in May, traveling the state to get a sense of the concerns of Louisiana residents. At the first stop, I didn't think anyone was going to show up, and the place was mobbed. "For those of you who don't know who I am," I said at one of the many lunch places I stopped in, "I'd suggest that you don't google that until you get home from work." It was a lot like going to clubs for feature dancing. I was honest, I showed up on time, and I was respectful of the people who came out to see me.

It was fun at first. People thought I was going to be an idiot, and here I was able to string a sentence together. "If you get any closer you're going to have to start tipping me," I told the reporters who hung on every zinger. The press interest gave me the opportunity to spew some stats I knew about the dangers of defunding sex education and the corresponding rise in rates of STDs and teen pregnancy. "If you don't want people to have the right to choose abortion," I said, "then you have to give them sex education. You can't have it both ways." And when I didn't know the answer, I didn't hide it. "Honestly, I'm a porn star, I don't know the answer to that question. Yet."

I thought it would just set the campaign up for someone else, but people started writing campaign checks, and I was going up in the polls. Vitter would not debate me or even acknowledge my existence, and I just loved that he was scared of me.

Still, I walked a very fine line of not trying to make a mockery of the process or appearing that I was only doing it to further my name. Yes, I did have a spike in my website views, but I didn't want to do a Senator Stormy video for Wicked.

One of my lines on the tour was "Politics can't be any dirtier of a job than the one I am already in." But I was wrong. I realized two weeks in that, just like the entertainment business but with way more repercussions, it's about who you know and it's about money. Vitter's war chest was estimated at two million dollars. Right there was the real civics lesson: The person most qualified to represent the average resident of his or her state could never afford to run. Which means they will never win. Which means the people will never have true representation. It's why we are stuck with a Congress full of millionaires. I started to get disheartened and was actually depressed for a while about that. Here I was, just doing this until an adult showed up, but what if there were no more honest grown-ups in politics?

Glen and I had continued talking every day for hours over the course of several weeks, leading up to the band's five-week tour of the United Kingdom and Europe. In the olden days of the summer of 2009, you couldn't use your American cell phone in Europe. He figured out we could do an audio version of a Skype call, and despite the time difference, we kept up with the daily calls. He would tell me where he was, Leeds and Wolverhampton in England, Glasgow in Scotland. I remember thinking that I knew someone who went on and on about Scotland, and then remembered Donald Trump and his stupid golf course. It didn't occur to me to mention him to Glen. Now that he'd finally stopped calling, Donald Trump was nowhere on my radar.

About three weeks into his overseas tour, Glen confessed something. "Would it be crazy if I told you that I missed you?" he asked.

We had only seen each other twice ever, and we hadn't even kissed. So, on paper, yes, file under crazy. But I missed him, too. "No," I said.

"Good, because I miss you," he said, sighing into the phone. "You should come to Europe."

"I'll come to Europe, don't tempt me."

It became like a dare. He clearly didn't think I would just hop on a plane to see him. But maybe he knew the best way to get me to do something is to tell me I can't.

I knew he was playing the last day of Pinkpop, a famous three-day festival held at Landgraaf in the Netherlands. Because it's outdoors, the venue can hold something like sixty thousand people, and Bruce Springsteen opened that weekend in 2009. Hollywood Undead were on the final night, Monday, June 1, on the tent stage with acts like the All-American Rejects and Katy Perry.

I hung up and bought a five-thousand-dollar plane ticket to Belgium. It was as close as I could get to Landgraaf, which can host such a big festival because it's in the middle of fucking nowhere. I danced Friday and Saturday nights in Pittsburgh, then sent my luggage home with my roadie and went directly from the club for a 6 A.M. flight.

My adrenaline and "I'll show you" energy had been pumping, so I didn't think about what I had done until they closed the cockpit doors. This was crazy for me. Christ, what if I got there and I just hated this guy? What if this was only working because it was all on the phone and all in my head? And then

I'd be trapped there for four days. On a bus with a band. What was I thinking?

When we landed in Brussels, I had a car pick me up to take me the hour-and-a-half drive to Landgraaf for the Pinkpop festival. It was only when I got out with my suitcase and saw this massive arena surrounded by a fence that I remembered one little detail: I didn't have a ticket. People pay hundreds of euros for tickets, and they buy them way in advance. The weekend was sold out, as it had been the year before and the year before that. But I had to get in there.

I scanned the area and spotted a low part of the fence. I threw my suitcase over, scaled the fence, and just took off running. I heard security behind me, yelling as they chased me.

I looked back as they were gaining on me, and I saw a golf cart racing toward me. At the wheel was Brian Pomp, who recognized me. Brian was the front-of-house engineer and, most important, owner of the only working cell at the festival.

"She's with the band!" he yelled, approaching me.

"I'm with the band!" I yelled back at them. Brian got to me before they did, quickly handing me a laminate. It was like a magic amulet, and I turned and held it up to the security guards. It was like I'd scaled the Berlin Wall, and I was safe now on the other side.

"Let me take you backstage, Stormy," Brian said. We drove there, and as we approached I saw that the stage was this huge open-air arena with about sixty thousand people already facing it. The "backstage" was a huge collection of temporary buildings, prefab cabins for each band and act. Musicians and crew were all hanging out in the summer sun, jamming and talking.

As Brian got closer to the Hollywood Undead cabin, Glen

and I spotted each other. He broke into a run when he saw me, and I jumped out to run toward him. He gave me the hugest hug, and right there in a place we'd never been, we kissed for the very first time.

We would make out so much over the next four days that at the end my lips were raw. The festival had the best vibe, and I just sat with him backstage as one superstar after another walked by. Katy Perry in a polka-dot summer dress, and the All-American Rejects, already practiced rock stars. Hollywood Undead played, and I got to see him work up close. There's nothing like watching him play drums. The band was never great or anything like that, but he is incredible.

Afterward, we went to the main stage to watch the last of the show. The headliner for the final night was Snow Patrol, a Northern Ireland band whose single "Chasing Cars" had been big in the States a few years before. But they had become absolutely huge in Europe. That year, "Chasing Cars" was named the most widely played song of the decade in the UK.

We got to stand down in front, in the wide VIP gap where security stands between the stage and sixty thousand screaming fans. The final song was "Chasing Cars," a pure love song inspired by something the lead singer's dad had said about some girl he was in love with. He was like a dog chasing a car, said his dad. He'd never catch it and wouldn't know what to do if he did.

We were standing there, the sun was just setting, it was getting dark. About three minutes in, as the song reached a crescendo, the singer let the audience sing for him. Behind us, sixty thousand people paid tribute to impossible love. "Would you lie with me," they all sang, "and just forget the world?"

Glen put his arms around me. It became, and would remain, our song.

I went on to the Amsterdam leg of Glen's tour, and the whole trip was magical from start to finish.

It was among the best four days of my life. I finally grew some balls and did something crazy. And it worked out.

I cannot say the same for my listening tour. I recommitted to it in July, giving it a try more out of obligation than desire to actually run. It was better than being in Tampa with Moz. I was doing more national interviews, to get myself excited about it again . . . and then my campaign manager's car got blown up.

Brian Welsh had parked his 1996 Audi convertible outside his apartment building in New Orleans the night of July 23. He and his wife were out walking their dog when the car exploded at eleven fifteen. I was told it was because of a Molotov cocktail, and Welsh posted a surveillance video that, sure enough, showed a person wearing a white shirt messing with the car shortly before it exploded in an action-film ball of flames. The New Orleans Fire Department didn't rule out foul play but said the car didn't technically explode. A small consolation, considering it looked like something you see on the news about Iraq.

"Clearly, if someone tried to blow up my car, it's cause for concern; it's not cause for me to stop doing my job, stop me from talking about the things that are important," Welsh told a reporter. Good for him, but I wasn't so sure I wanted to continue if it meant my car could be next. I went home to Tampa to think about it and walked into a different kind of trap.

The afternoon of Saturday, July 25, I got to my house, which was always a cute little house even if I was stuck with Moz in it. It was a two-thousand-and-change-square-foot two-story with a porch and palm trees out front. I walked in around three o'clock to discover that Moz's dad had been over earlier and once again chosen to do my laundry. That sounds like a nice gesture, but let's just say that in the past I had repeatedly told Moz that I was creeped out by his dad repeatedly going into our hamper and touching my dirty underwear. I didn't even want Moz touching my underwear anymore, let alone his dad. So, when I realized it had happened again, I was pissed.

That was what set me off, and I yelled at Moz about it. Making matters much worse, I opened some bills that hadn't been paid, only to realize that a bunch of money was missing out of our bank account. I threw a potted plant hard into the sink, to water it or maybe just to make a point that I was tired of all this and I wanted to start my new life without him. Yes, it hit the sink hard, but it was away from Moz.

I could feel the rage building in me—I am serious about my underwear and my money—so I wanted to leave. And Moz didn't want me to. He had my car keys, holding them high over his head when I lunged for them. When I tried to get them from him, he said I hit his head. Maybe, but it certainly wasn't my intention. I wanted to get the fuck out of there.

He then walked into the living room like it was some sort of game, and I followed him. I knocked over our wedding album from the coffee table, which in turn knocked over two shitty candles I never liked anyway. And Moz, this publicist who had drilled into me the Hollywood rule that you never let police get ahold of the story before your PR has had a chance to spin it, suddenly decided to call the police.

And here came his new friends, the cops, rolling up to the house. They took a look at this guy, five foot nine and weighing in at 175 pounds, and arrested me for domestic violence. "I observed the victim to have no physical injuries, marks, or scratches on his body," Officer DeSouza writes in the police report. "His demeanor was calm and very friendly." Of course it was. I could have easily lied and said he hit me, but I would never, ever do something like that.

There are little check marks on police reports to help officers assess your attitude. I got all nos on "Alcohol Consumed," "Fearful," "Threatening," "Uncooperative," and—thank God—"Pregnant." Next to "Angry," you bet there's a check mark. Oh, yeah, and on "Crying," but it's hard for me to admit that.

They took me to central booking at Hillsborough County jail, and they got their mug shot. There were no charges pressed, and I was free to go, but that mug shot sure was convenient to run on all the stories that focused on what a setback this was to my potential campaign. All the outlets hyping the story made note that I was "upset because of the way the laundry had been done," but curiously left out my estranged publicist husband's dad going into my hamper to get my dirty underwear. I never went back to that house again.

Between my campaign manager's car going up in flames and me getting arrested so my mug shot would be everywhere, I got the message. I ended the listening tour and called off the campaign. But I wanted to make one final point in my statement. "The simple fact that David Vitter has five million dollars in his bank account pretty much says it all. Against that sheer accumulation of special-interest dollars, I have no legitimate means of winning a race for the United States Senate. . . . I am

not not running for the U.S. Senate because I am an adult entertainment star. I am not running for the U.S. Senate for the
same reason that so many dedicated patriots do not run—I
can't afford it."

Flash forward to where those men in my life ended up: Vitter
won, of course. He went on to vote to defund Planned Parenthood and block a rare bipartisan energy bill—which promised to
reduce the nation's energy costs by four billion dollars and slow
climate change. He unsuccessfully ran for governor in 2015 and
decided not to run for reelection. In March 2018, he registered
as a lobbyist for Cajun Industries LLC, a construction company
run by Lane Grigsby, a megadonor to conservative candidates
and causes. Two months earlier, President Trump had nominated Vitter's virulently antichoice wife, Wendy, to be a judge
in the U.S. District Court for the Eastern District of Louisiana.
During her hearing in April, Wendy refused to answer whether
she thought *Brown v. Board of Ed*—the 1954 case in which the
Supreme Court ruled unanimously that racial segregation in
public schools violated the Fourteenth Amendment—had gone
the right way. But I'm the sicko.

As for Moz, he dragged out the divorce, fighting over everything and refusing to just sign the papers. I just wanted to be
done with him, and one time I point-blank asked him: "Why
are you being such a pain in the ass about this?"

"You're my wife and you're staying that way," he said. Spoiler
alert: I didn't.

Serial monogamist that I am, Glen and I immediately got together as I extricated myself from Moz. He told me he had a

place in L.A. that he crashed at when he wasn't on tour. I wanted to see him, so I scheduled an L.A. shoot for when he would have some time off. He got there a few days before me, and every time I called him I would ask what he was doing. The answer was always the same: he was either walking to Subway or coming back from there. Around the fourth time, I thought, *This motherfucker loves sandwiches.*

"How many sandwiches are you gonna eat?" I finally asked him.

"Not Subway. *The* subway."

"L.A. has a subway?"

It does—who knew? Glen lived like a kid who happened to be a rock star. He had no car and, as I would find out, no real apartment. He just rented a room from some chick down one of the side streets across from the Guitar Center in Hollywood. "There's no reason for me to get a place of my own because I'm gone all the time," he assured me. But he also warned me that his roommate was "kinda" weird.

What he did not tell me was that when you got to this apartment, as I did the night before my shoot, you opened the door to a living room with nothing in it except a *giant* hot-pink papier-mâché squid. Its long, foot-wide tentacles were everywhere, climbing up the walls and resting on windows. It had suction cups about the size of my fist.

"She adds to it when she's high," Glen said.

I had so many questions. I still have so many questions. But I escaped the sea creature and got to his room. He had a mattress on the floor, a skateboard, a drum kit, and some clothes in a box. Nothing else, certainly not an air conditioner. I stayed over, and all through the night people threw bottles in the

Dumpster right by his window. In the morning I showered after Glen showed me how to use pliers to turn the water on.

One night was enough for me. "I'm out," I said, "and you're coming with me. We're gonna rent you an apartment."

The new place became one of our landing pads when we weren't on the road. Glen respected my job and never asked me about my past relationships. It never once occurred to me to say to Glen: "Guess what I did one time? I fucked Donald Trump." Who gives their partner a laundry list of the people they've had sex with?

But I admit I was intensely curious about his. Not out of jealousy, but this was the first grown person I had been with who was not from the porn world. He had slept with—let's be real—fucked loads of women on tour. He would tell me what he did with girls, and I would have to stop him like a sheltered anthropologist of sex.

"Wait, what?" I remember saying. "You didn't know this girl and she just grabbed your dick? People do that in real life?"

He described things that maybe I hadn't done on camera but certainly had directed in porn, but I thought it was all just fantasy. Tales of women wanting double penetration in a threesome or demanding that he cum on their face.

"You are *joking*," I would say. He thought it was funny that I was so ignorant about what happened in the real world, but everything I learned about sex was from working in porn. I didn't even know how to have a one-night stand. I could not imagine walking up to someone in a bar and saying, "Can I suck your cock? Meet me out back." But this had happened to Glen! Out there in the straight world. I couldn't get my head around it and I still can't, to be honest.

As I pressed for more details about life in the real world, he let slip about one person he slept with who I never expected: my friend Amanda. Yes, the one who thought he was too dirty to even get in her car the night I met him.

"What?" I yelled, way, way more out of surprise than annoyance. "She hated you! You fucked her?"

"Maybe I didn't," he said. "I remember her kissing me and then I woke up and she was in bed with me."

"You totally fucked her!"

I didn't blame either of them. They didn't think I had any intention of dating him. Soon after that I was in Tampa and I bumped into her on a night out networking. She was having a drink, and she put her phone down on the bar to give me a hug.

"How's it going?" she said.

"I'm just in town for a little bit," I said. "I'm just back from touring with Hollywood Undead." I said it very pointedly to see her reaction.

"Oh yeah, that band," she said. "I forgot. So, uh, you still talk to that guy?"

"Yeah," I said. "Do you?"

"No, why would I do that? Though, you know, I think I ended up in his room that night. . . ."

"Yeah?" I said.

"Yeah, but it was totally no big deal," she said, smoothing her hair. "I actually forgot about the whole thing until you mentioned him."

"Cool," I said.

"Cool," she said.

We sat there, and just as it couldn't get more awkward, her

phone rang. And her ringtone was a song from Hollywood Undead.

I wanted to laugh so hard, but I just smiled at her.

"Um, I'm, uh . . . ," she said, snatching her phone, "I'm gonna take this outside."

As with *almost* everything that happened in my life, I couldn't wait to tell Glen.

SIX

You know I wasn't that kid who played Mommy with dolls. I just never had that urge to to be a parent when I grew up. I was going to be a rock star, or at least live like one. Besides, you can't ride a horse if you're pregnant, so who would want that? Then my body obviously became a big part of my career, and let's face it, that shit just looks like it fucking hurts. In fact, childbirth is the worst idea anyone's ever had.

And then, once I was with Glen, the idea started creeping up on me. It continued to grow once we moved to our new place in Las Vegas. There were a lot of kids around, and I would have a weird feeling when I saw them. Was it maternal instinct? Gas?

I put it out of my mind until one morning when Glen and I were at home. I was on the couch, writing up a script on my laptop. Glen came in like he'd had a revelation.

"I want to have a kid," he said.

"Ha, ha," I said. "No." I went back to typing.

"Serious," he said.

The thought hung there in the space between us, just long enough for me to formulate a plan.

"Okay," I said. "But there are terms. You have to do porn."

"Uh, what?" He laughed. Poor guy thought I was joking.

"If I let you get me pregnant," I said, "*you* have to do porn."

"Well, why? That doesn't make any sense."

"Because if we ever split up, you can't use it against me in court."

"Well, I would never . . ."

I laughed ruefully and closed the laptop. "One, everybody says that," I said. "Two, it might not even be your decision." I have had friends in the adult entertainment business who have had their kids taken away from them by judges who don't approve of their careers. These were instances where the mother and father were splitting amicably and had agreed on everything regarding custody, but the judge vetoed it. The decision, which was out of the hands of the parents, amounted to "Oh, she's a whore. You get the kid." I know a couple who doesn't even follow the custody agreement, but if something happened the mom would be screwed.

"Let's just level the playing field," I continued. "So you can't say I can't have the kid because I did porn." I have always been a realist. I was very aware of what men are capable of doing to hurt the women they once loved.

"That is so fucked up, Stormy," he said, "but you're kind of a genius."

"I love you, too," I said. "So those are my terms. Take it or leave it."

"Well, I don't know if I can," he said. "What if I'm not good at it?"

"That's also a good point," I said. "The only way to know is if you try."

So we started slow. I asked Keith to shoot a photo set for my website. That went great, so we did a scene with him filming us having sex as a POV thing. I didn't throw him in the deep end.

Then I added him into scenes of some of the smaller films I was directing and always had him doing scenes with just me. One of the first was called *Whatever It Takes,* funnily enough. I never critiqued his work in front of people but trained him at home. The sex is completely different. Sex at home is about what feels good; sex on camera is about what looks good. Especially for the woman.

I then "graduated" him to doing a couple of bigger movies with me, which meant that he had a lot more dialogue and was more integral to the story. Glen killed it because he's such a great actor. It's a testament to him that he did so well, because I know I am really hard to do a scene with if I'm directing. I can feel the camera move down my body, and as soon as it's off my face, I'm craning my head to look at the monitor.

This was strictly an insurance policy if we broke up, not about guaranteeing two incomes. He only shot for me, so that $600 or $700 he got paid amounted to $150 or $200 by the time I bought his plane tickets and paid the $200 just to have his STD test done. We probably did seven or eight movies when Glen said, "Okay, I did it. So we're good to go."

"No way," I said.

"But I did porn."

"You can always stand up in court and be like, 'She did a hundred scenes in her career, and on the few that I did, I only worked with her.'"

"So what do you want?" he asked.

"You need to fuck other bitches." He rolled his eyes. I was sex-trafficking my husband.

I cast him in *Love in an Elevator* and gave him the superhot Kirsten Price as his scene partner. This guy managed to go laterally to another Wicked contract star. He only ever worked with A-list girls, which is astounding compared to the career trajectories of other male performers. You have a hundred guys a day approaching agents saying, "I wanna be a porn star." Unless you have a hot girl saying, "I only want to do my scenes with him," the only way guys really get in is by starting at the very bottom. Guy #57 in the two-hundred-guy gang bang. Or starting in gay porn and switching over.

And so, I got pregnant with a baby girl. All because my husband had sex with other women while I watched and worried about their makeup and angles so they'd look their best.

I was instantly fat. I know girls whose tummies don't pop out until they're like six months along. Six *hours* after conception, it was like, "Yup, she's pregnant."

I had terrible morning sickness, but in all honesty, I didn't mind being pregnant. Mostly because I didn't have to work. The pregnancy was planned, and I did twice as much work the year before so I wouldn't have to perform. And when I directed, I just sat in a chair as the crew fawned over me and brought me food. It's not like I was going through what so many women in this country do, getting up and working five days a week at some job doing manual labor until their due date. I had it very cushy. Though I do remember a time when I was heavily pregnant and on the floor as Glen raised a leg over me so I could shave his taint before a scene. "Is this rock bottom?" I said aloud, genuinely asking the universe.

Glen still had to work hard, though. Some days more than others. He was doing a movie for me and had a scene with a woman I will never name, and you know I can keep secrets. He was doing promotional stills with her in another room when he came tiptoeing in, bashfully covering his dick. I was sitting in a chair, eating a plate of chocolate cake someone had brought the nice pregnant director.

"I don't think I can do it," he whispered.

I stopped eating, but only for a second. It was good cake. "What the fuck do you mean you can't do it?" I said. I had written this big feature with a role tailored to him and he had already been established with two days of dialogue.

"Uh, she has hair in her nose," he said.

"Then don't look at her nose," I said. "Fuck her doggy."

He leaned in, smacking his lips like he'd tasted something bad. "Pussy's a little gamy," he whispered.

I lost it. I growled at him in a voice out of *The Exorcist*. "You get in there and you fuck that pretty girl and you make me some money."

He slunk off and did just that. He did so well that as the scene was building to the climax she called out his character's name and yelled "I love you." At those words, Glen broke character and looked right in the camera with a mortified expression.

"Cut!" I yelled, furious that they'd blown the take.

Husbands, am I right?

Full disclosure: I gained ninety-three pounds while I was pregnant. I gained a full-size human in addition to my little baby. I mean, the physics of it were outstanding, with my huge tits and growing belly. I didn't know your body could get that big.

My due date was Halloween 2011, which meant I was pregnant

all summer in hot-as-hell Vegas. My solution to any discomfort was mostly to lie in bed and get super addicted to bad TV. I watched things that I would never watch now, *like it was a job.* When I hear people saying they binge-watched a show they DVRed, I think, *Amateur.*

Not me. I made a schedule with a chart of what shows were on. I even mapped out what to do if two of my shows were on at the same time—which to watch live and which to DVR in the other room. MTV's reality shows *Sixteen and Pregnant* and *Teen Mom* were my absolute favorites because we were in it together. Those original Teen Moms, by the way, those are my girls. We did this together. I'm fifteen years older than them, but that's beside the point.

Hoarders and *Labor and Delivery* were appointment television for me, as were reruns of the E! series *Pretty Wild,* about delightfully self-obsessed sisters, one of whom is part of the Bling Ring accused of robbing homes of celebrities like Orlando Bloom and Paris Hilton.

I didn't watch *Jersey Shore.* I had *some* standards.

And when I was settled in for my programs, I needed my ice cream. My drug of choice was Ben & Jerry's Strawberry Cheesecake. It has these beautiful pink chunks of strawberry and wedges of pie-crust-like cookie—heaven. I'd never had it before my pregnant body demanded it, and I haven't had a bite of it since. But at around five months, I started eating a pint every night. Glen would have to go out and buy me *one,* because if he bought two or three, I would eat two or three. He would gradually buy out the stock in each of the stores by our house, slowly expanding his radius farther and farther until they replenished and he could start again.

One night, he was gone for a really long time. So long that I wondered not just *Where is my fucking ice cream?* but *Is he okay?*

Finally, he came rushing in the door with the ice cream. When I saw him, all my concern evaporated, and it went right back to the anger of a pregnant woman who'd been kept waiting. *"What took you so long?"* I snapped at him.

"I had to go all the way to the Walmart Neighborhood Market," he said.

"Why'd you go so far?"

"Babe, you've eaten all . . ." He caught himself. "The stores around us aren't good on inventory."

I didn't answer, just peeled off the plastic ring wrap and felt the satisfying release of the cardboard coming away from the ice cream. *We can talk later,* I thought.

"I got there and there was one left," he continued, a tiny amount of fear sneaking into his voice. "And just as I was reaching for it, an old lady got it before me."

My eyes got big as I took a second dive with my spoon.

"Then," he continued, with shame replacing the fear, "I followed her around the store for fifteen minutes until she wasn't looking. I stole it out of her cart."

He had done the right thing, but still I wondered. "Why didn't you just ask her for it?" I asked. "A woman might understand."

"Yeah, but what if she said, 'Go fuck yourself,' and I had to fight an old lady for it?" he asked. "Oh, God, I just stole ice cream out of an old lady's shopping cart."

"Thank you, babe," I said.

He kissed my head and sighed. "The only thing more terrifying than stealing ice cream from an old lady," he said, "was coming home without it."

Poor Glen, I had so many cravings. They weren't weird like pickles, they were just extremely specific and, uh, time sensitive. To have it immediately was almost too late. The act of eating was enough of a middleman, thank you. Early on, I needed green beans, but that seemed easy.

Canned, fresh, I didn't care. Later, Glen would know to just get whatever I craved and throw it my way, but we were new to this and he wanted me to have the best green beans. It was a day we were leaving Vegas to go to L.A. because he had a show.

"I know the best place to get green beans," he said, so proud of himself. "Peggy Sue's." Peggy Sue's 50's Diner is in Yermo, California, almost exactly halfway between Vegas and L.A. "You know you're going to have to pee halfway there," he said. "I bet you they have fucking amazing green beans."

"I'm in!" I yelled.

As we drove through the desert, I just kept thinking about those green beans. As we got off the I-15 freeway, I could taste them. Peggy Sue's is so cute, an original 1950s roadside diner made to look like you went through a time warp. I could not have cared less in the moment. I ran to the bathroom to pee, then squeezed into a booth.

The waitress came over, all done up like 1954, wearing a turquoise waitress uniform with pink trim and a matching cap and apron.

"What can I get you, hon?" she asked.

"I'll have the meat loaf, with mashed potatoes, and . . ." I paused, like everyone knew what I was about to say. ". . . the green beans, please."

"We just ran out of green beans," she said.

She said it so nonchalantly. Going so entirely off-script that the director in me wanted to fire her on the spot. Instead, I burst into tears. Huge, face-to-the-ceiling, bawling tears. I was sitting in the middle of the desert crying my eyes out because I felt so pregnant and all I wanted was green beans.

The waitress looked at Glen and said, "She must really like green beans."

He nodded and asked for a minute. Glen came over to my side of the booth and held me. "I know," he said. "I know."

We decided early on that we were going to have a home water birth with a midwife. I don't think that pregnancy is a condition, and I don't want to go to a hospital full of germs unless there's a reason. I also heard something horrible: hospitals don't let you eat or drink during labor. Fuck your ice chips, I was doing this at home. We interviewed midwives and we found a lady that I instantly connected with and liked, Sherry. Our plan was that she would be there as an adviser, and Glen would deliver our girl in our tub. The best-laid plans . . .

Sherry gave us a list of things we needed to have for our home birthing kit. Glen took on the job of getting everything on the list. Sterile gloves and things like that. He would come home every day with something, and he'd proudly cross it off the list.

I can't remember what the very last thing was, but when he brought it home, he showed it to me, then pulled out a small green aquarium net on a stick. "And I got *this*!"

"That wasn't on the list," I said. "The baby is not a fish, and she's not going to fit in that."

"It's in case you poop in the water!" he said, so proud.

Every range of emotion crossed my face in three seconds. It

went from "Ooooh, how ingenious," to "Oh, God," disgusted, to "Awww, he is so sweet," and then horrified that my husband even knew I was capable of pooping. Because we were not that couple. I'd never even heard Glen fart or burp. We believed in separate bathrooms, so outside of sex, our bodily functions were mysterious to each other. The thought that I might poop in front of him, and possibly on him if he's in the tub with me—Oh, God. It scared me to a point where I thought, *Okay, maybe we won't do this.* But then I remembered the "no food" hospital rule and decided this was worth the risks.

My dignity requests that I tell you this is the last we will speak of the net, because it would never be used, thank you.

We were all set in the weeks leading up to our baby girl's October 31 due date. And then Halloween passed. And then the next day. Then a week. I was as big as a house and had no one to blame but me, but now my ice cream baby didn't want to come out. My friends told me I needed to schedule an induction, but I didn't want to go that route. "This baby's going to come out with a driver's license," I said.

We tried everything to get her out. Pregnancy massage, acupuncture, spicy food, sex. None of it worked. *Two weeks* went by and there was still no baby. Finally, a really good sale put me into labor. We were walking around the Las Vegas North Premium Outlets, an outdoor mall near our house. I got really excited over a two-for-one sale on Juicy Couture leggings. I felt a cramp, and I'd never had any false labor pains, so I knew it was go time.

When we got home it was about five in the afternoon, and by eight o'clock the contractions were every three minutes. We called the midwife and she rushed over in her minivan. I went from zero to seven centimeters in about five hours, so they thought it would be quick. "You'll have this baby before midnight," Sherry said.

I thought so, too. From my tub, I could see a high window in the bathroom. I watched the sun go down, I watched the sun come up. I watched the sun go down, I watched the sun come up.

Two days of contractions, every three to five minutes without a break, and no baby.

I tried walking, I tried lying down. I couldn't sleep and was so nauseous from pain, I couldn't eat. I would take a sip of Gatorade and throw up two sips' worth. Sherry kept checking the baby's heart rate, and she was totally fine. It never dipped, and she wasn't in distress. So we kept trying.

They broke my water for me with a needle. It sounds like it would hurt, but it just feels like you just peed on yourself. That didn't work, and I was still stuck at seven centimeters. Glen slept here and there, and finally I slept in the tub. Sherry took a photo of Glen and me both asleep. I'm in the tub, of course, my head on the side, and Glen is curled up on the bath rug. We're holding hands, even in sleep.

I woke at about 2 A.M. The midwife had gone downstairs to lie on the couch in the guest room. Glen was still sleeping on the mat. I was enormous in the water, and in between contractions, I looked down. I will never forget this moment: my belly churned, went completely flat, and then stuck out again.

"Glen!" I screamed. "Glen. Glen. Get Sherry." He raced out of the room, and I couldn't stop shaking.

Sherry came up and was very calm. "Step out of the water," she said, "and let me check you." She knelt to examine the baby's positioning, and as I remember the half-second that a look came over her face, I have to stop typing to collect myself. It was puzzlement, concern, and then real stark fear before she managed to hide it.

"We gotta go to the hospital," she said.

"What?"

My baby had had enough. She had backed up and flipped herself over to a breech position. "If this doesn't work," I imagine her saying on some primal level, "I'm coming out feetfirst."

"I am calling it," Sherry said. "You can still have the baby naturally, but I am calling it. We have to go. You have been in labor for forty-eight hours and your water's been broken for twenty-four hours. We're going."

There is nothing like being in full-blown labor and you're leaking and your husband is trying to put a diaper on you and dress you. Sherry wanted a bucket to put under me in the car, but all we had was a popcorn bowl. They waddle-walked me out to the car. I was so dehydrated and out of it, but I had one moment of clarity when they opened the door to my Escalade.

"Not in my Escalade," I yelled to Sherry. "We're taking your minivan."

We three burst out laughing. "This is an eighty-thousand-dollar vehicle," I said. "I am not giving birth in it."

So there I was in a minivan, sitting over this bowl.

"IF I HAVE THIS BABY IN A POPCORN BOWL IN A MINIVAN . . . ," I yelled as we raced to the hospital. "I WORKED SO HARD TO GET OUT OF LOUISIANA. YOU ARE NOT GOING TO DRAG ME BACK TO MY ROOTS."

We got to the hospital at close to 3 A.M. And this is important for the world to know: the intake nurse at St. Rose Hospital was a fucking bitch. Lady, please come to a book signing and stand in line so that when you get to me I can call you a bitch to your face. She gave us attitude because we weren't preregistered at the hospital and made it as clear as possible that she was not a home-birth supporter.

I was already terrified, but now I was worried that I was going to deliver this baby with a doctor that I had never met before. And in walks Dr. Steven Harter, the most sought-after obstetrician in Las Vegas. With his pro-mom approach and amazing bedside manner, women plan their entire births around his availability. And here he was, on rotation that night.

"We think that you are too tired to push and your body knows that," Dr. Harter told me. "Because if it finished dilating, you won't have the strength to get the baby out. So, your labor is stalling. Here's what we're gonna do. We're going to give you an epidural so you don't feel anything, which just means you can take a nap. You won't feel your contractions, and I bet when you wake up you'll be refreshed and ready to push."

"Okay," I said, "sounds great."

The anesthesiologist came in to give me the epidural, and Glen's face went white at the sight of the needle. The anesthesiologist put it in, and the pain went away immediately. I was so thankful, I tried to kiss the anesthesiologist.

Thirty seconds after my pain completely went away, hunger pangs started, as if my stomach was going to rip itself open. I hadn't eaten for two and a half days, and the epidural couldn't mask that. There was no way I could sleep when I was this hungry. A nurse happened to come in to ask if there was anything she could do for me.

"I'm starving," I said. "Is there some food—"

"You can't have anything to eat," she scolded. She said something else, but all I heard was "Blah blah blah ice chips." And she left.

I waited until that door closed.

"Glen, come here," I said. "Closer." I reached up my hand, as if to gently touch his face, and I grabbed him by the throat.

"*Vending machine. Now.*"

"But she said . . ."

I tightened my grip. "Okay," he croaked out.

He came back with an armful of stuff. "I didn't know what you wanted," he said. "Pick what you want."

"Yes," I said, grabbing everything.

I ate everything and then passed out. Glen immediately fell asleep in a chair across from me because he was so exhausted, too. Two hours later, in came the nasty intake nurse.

She pulled back my covers and shrieked. I was *covered* in crumbs and wrappers.

"*WHAT?*" I said, with all the menace I could muster. "What?"

She huffed and walked out, saying she was going to tell the doctor. Snitch. Dr. Harter came in and was cool about it. "It's fine," he said. "You've been through a lot." He checked my cervix and there was still no progression. He told me the only thing they could do was give me Pitocin. I had been against inducing, which is what Pitocin is all about, but I was willing to try anything at that point. Besides, every hour I was at the hospital, I was running up a bill. All I was hearing was cha-ching, cha-ching.

At seven in the morning there was still no progress, so I scheduled the C-section. Now, I already told you that I was paranoid about being in a hospital. I have to tell you that I also had an irrational fear that someone was going to give me the wrong baby. Judge all you want, but that's the kind of thing that would happen to me. I knew it takes like a minute to get the baby out and twenty minutes to get you back together, so I made Glen promise that when they took the baby out of the operating room, he had to go with her.

Fun fact: when they give you a C-section, most doctors strap your arms down. Dr. Harter said he could take the straps off, thank God. "You promise you're not going to sit up and reach down and pull out your own organs or punch me in the face?"

"I promise," I said.

Glen had his camera and filmed the whole thing. It is graphic as fuck and it took me a long time to watch it. It's very . . . red.

Dr. Harter had his iPod going during the surgery and was rocking out to Led Zeppelin. The moment my daughter was born, Alanis Morissette's "Thank U" filled the room. Once again, Alanis was there with just the right song at just the right moment. Dr. Harter pulled her out and said, "Oh, boy!"

"What?" I said. "It's a girl, right?"

"Oh, yeah," he said. "She's just so big."

He handed her off to the nurses, and they took her over to a warming cart to weigh her. She was almost nine pounds and long, twenty-three inches. But the room was very, very quiet, with only Alanis singing.

The baby wasn't crying.

I know from the video that the nurses looked quizzical and started rubbing the baby. Glen put the camera down. In the video, you just see the floor and only hear us talking.

"Wha—what's wrong?" he says. "Something wrong?"

They don't answer but focus on rubbing her.

"Step back for a second, sir," says a nurse.

"What's wrong?" Glen asks again.

"WHAT'S WRONG?" you hear me scream.

Our baby let out the smallest cry.

"All right, she's good," says the doctor.

Then my husband let out the biggest cry. Glen, who had stood by me through all this, who had been so scared for me and for her, broke.

You just hear him sobbing on the video, sputtering out, "She's—" *Sob.* "So—" *Sob.* "Beautiful."

It sounded so funny and ridiculous that I slapped my hand to my forehead. As soon as he left with the baby and two of the nurses, the remaining nurses broke into laughter. I started to laugh and they had to yell at me. "Stop laughing!" one said. "Stuff is gonna fly out of you."

"Well," said the doctor, "he's an emotional guy."

"Yeah," I said. "He feels things."

"All right, look," he said, conspiratorially. "I made your incision especially low and very small. I'm going to take extra time closing it up."

"Oh, thank you," I said.

Dr. Harter smiled. "I'm gonna have you back in front of the camera in no time."

I had never told him who I was, but he recognized me. I smiled back at him. And yes, I have the best C-section scar. I love my fans.

SEVEN

At first, I figured it had to be about the cigarettes. Glen quit smoking the day our daughter was born, so maybe that was the problem. Then I thought it was lack of sleep and the stress of being a parent to a newborn after a traumatic delivery—all of those things are very normal. Because within the first few days of her life, Glen went completely, well, insane.

I like to say I didn't get postpartum depression, but he did. He wasn't sleeping, which wasn't really so much because of our having a baby in the house, because she was such a good sleeper from the beginning. I remember standing by her crib, whispering, "For the love of God, wake up! My tits are gonna explode."

Glen would appear manic, starting a project and leaving it unfinished because he moved on to another one. "Sit down, Glen," I said countless times, "you're making me nervous." He would look at her and start crying and get emotional.

Finally, he broke down. "I always had a problem with the fact that my dad never said 'I love you,'" he told me. "Now that I have her, and I look at her, I can't imagine why a parent wouldn't tell a child that they loved them. I can't imagine a day going by without saying it to her. So I am going to make sure I tell her every single day that I love her."

(Now she is like, "I get it." Because he tells her a hundred times a day. There will never be a doubt in my mind that my daughter knows her father loves her.)

Glen's intense love and adoration for our perfect baby girl brought up painful memories from his childhood. He was having what he thought were nightmares, which were triggered by seeing how vulnerable our daughter was, and he coped by using alcohol. He told me he felt unworthy of having a family. He was drinking all day every day and having a lot of problems with his band.

And I had a newborn and I'd gained ninety-three pounds. I was still leaking out of everywhere, and I had had the whole plan that I would deliver naturally—not two weeks late by cesarean—and do some miracle snapback in time to be at the January AVN Awards, my industry's version of the Oscars.

In the middle of this shit blizzard, my phone rang. I was holding my daughter in our living room, probably wearing the same shirt I'd worn yesterday.

"Daniels. Spears. Wassup?"

I recognized Randy Spears's voice immediately. He had been at Wicked during the Trump time. He had recently left the business, but had married and then divorced a woman who was a porn veteran, Gina Rodriguez. She's found her real calling as an entertainment manager with a specialty for handling mistresses, secret sexters, and D-listers looking to either extend their fifteen minutes of fame or at least get a payoff. Her big break was the slew of Tiger Woods mistresses selling their sexts and stories to the highest tabloid bidders.

"Hey, so I was just talking about you and somehow it came up," he said, "that you knew Donald Trump."

I rolled my eyes but said nothing. *Somehow.* I really liked Randy, but it did me no good to talk.

"Gina wants to talk to you about it," he said. Glen was outside, and I didn't want to risk having this conversation in front of him.

"I'm really not—"

This bright voice came on. "You know, I could probably help you tell your story."

"No, I am not interested."

"Well, my partner Gloria Allred wants to talk to you."

"Who is that?"

I was probably the only person on the planet who didn't know who this person was. I know now that she's a lawyer who specializes in high-profile cheating and harassment scandals. She worked with Gina on presenting Joslyn James as a former mistress seeking an apology from Tiger Woods for leading her on.

"Look her up," Gina said. "I gave her your number."

Sure enough, Gloria Allred called me. I was folding baby clothes in the living room. My daughter was on her back on a blanket next to me, and I sent Glen out on a Walmart run.

"Okay, what's your story?" Gloria said.

I paused. I wanted to tell her that I was an accomplished star, writer, and director of adult films, plus I had just had a baby who was clearly exceptional because I had seen other brats in my day.

And my hot husband was going through a lot, but I loved him and he adored our child. Oh, and I had to lose ninety-three pounds because the AVN Awards, my industry's biggest night of the year, was in a couple of weeks and those bitches were just waiting for me to roll in. Meanwhile, yes, I was still leaking out of places.

But I knew she didn't care about that.

I barreled through an extremely abbreviated version of my interactions with Donald Trump, leaving out sex and anything in the least bit interesting.

"Is there anything more?" she asked.

"No," I said, putting a finger close to my daughter's hand so she could hold it.

"Well, I really can't do anything for you if that's all there is."

"Sorry," I said.

I hung up and that was that, right? A couple of months went by, and I was still trying to lose the weight and fully recover so I could go back to work. I did two years' worth of work in one year in anticipation of being out of commission for a while, but I hadn't counted on my daughter being late and me needing a cesarean.

In March 2011, I got another call from Gina. "Oh, my God," she said, panic in her voice. "Have you seen the internet?"

That seemed so strange. Like she was asking if I was familiar with this new and exciting invention where people can find facts and naked pictures.

"What are you talking about?" I asked.

"There's a story about you and Trump on *The Dirty*," she said.

"The what?"

"*The Dirty*," she said. "It's a gossip site."

"How is there a story about me on there?"

"Don't worry," she said. "Do you want me to ask my attorney to have it removed?"

"What are you talking about? What does it say?" I went over to my computer and was trying to find it online when she started reading it to me, saying I had had an affair with Trump. It said a friend leaked it.

"So, do you want my attorney, Keith Davidson, to send them a letter?"

"YES!" I yelled. It seemed perfect. My only thought was, *This needs to go away.* Glen was a mess, I was a mess—we were in no position to suddenly have a spotlight on us.

The story was down in a couple of hours. Now that I have seen so many incorrect things about me printed and posted, I realize that is fast. *Extremely* fast.

That's how Keith Davidson entered my life. I didn't know that Davidson's specialty was brokering sex tapes and the like. At the time, it just seemed like I'd been saved from humiliation. Glen was not going to be looking at a gossip website I had never heard of. I had shut it down.

It was quiet, and I went back to the work of getting in shape. Twice a week, I did MamaFit workout classes, where I could take my daughter with me. I was trying to put Humpty Dumpty back together again. I was also trying to help Glen get his life back in order. He'd been through a lot and was starting to think he would benefit from professional help. Which costs money, which meant I had to get back to work.

Just a couple of weeks after Keith and Gina came to my

rescue taking down the story from *The Dirty,* I got a call from *In Touch.* And now they had the story. This stranger on the phone told me *my* story. They had about 80 percent of the details and made it all a little more sensational around the edges. Like a romance novel version of some hot and heavy affair. *Um, are you into sharks?* I thought.

"I have no comment," I said. "I'm not talking."

"Well, we're going to run the story anyway," I recall the person saying. "So, you have two options: You can either tell us the story in your words and get compensated for it. Or we'll run the version we have, which may or may not be accurate, and someone else gets the money."

"I don't . . ." I said.

"Well, think about it."

Who was this "someone else" telling my story? People think I approached *In Touch* with the story, but I never would have done that. I called Gina in a panic, and she put it in my head that it was my ex-husband Mike Moz. He did seem like a good candidate, and I 100 percent believed her at the time. He was smart enough to have come up with the plan, and he had about 80 percent of the story. It all pointed directly to him.

"I could get you fifteen thousand dollars for this story," Gina said. "Do you really want to hand him fifteen grand?"

"Well, no."

"It's going to come out anyway, so you might as well have control over it and compensation," she said. "We can make a ton of money and you can have them make the check out to your daughter."

We were running out of money and nothing had worked

the way it was supposed to. And also, my feeling was *Fuck you, Mike Moz.* I didn't want him profiting off my life any more than he already had.

I agreed to do an interview, which I did over the phone. I talked about Trump's promise to get me on *The Apprentice* but left out his plan to help me once I was on the show. We talked for an hour to this nice girl who asked me things like "Was the sex romantic?" I know even she has been in the media echo chamber, repeatedly telling her story about me telling my story, but I wouldn't remember her name if you put a gun to my head. When that was done, I got another call from an editor at *In Touch.*

"You know, this writer put this together," said the editor, "and it seems so far-fetched. Is this real?"

"Yeah." What seemed so far-fetched? Was it the spanking? Shark Week? That I had a brain?

"Well, you're gonna have to take a lie detector test."

"Are you calling me a liar?"

"We'd like to be sure."

"Fuck, yeah," I said, because I hate being called a liar. Later that month, I went to take a lie detector test, and a polygraph expert named Ron Slay asked me about a hundred questions. He later submitted a sworn statement that read like a report card. "Ms. Clifford presented herself well in outward appearance of credibility," said Slay. "There were no observable indications of intent to deceive." And then the money shot: "In the opinion of this examiner Ms. Clifford is truthful about having unprotected vaginal intercourse with Donald Trump in July 2006." Ding, ding, ding—told ya I wasn't a liar.

Gina called. She was cooking up a plan. "Let this *In Touch* thing come out," she said, "and then you're going to go quiet and everyone's going to be trying to take a picture of you."

"Oh, God, no," I said.

"And then we can sell a photo shoot of you."

"*No* photo shoots of me," I said. "I look so bad."

Gina wasn't listening. She was excited about all the TV shows she was going to shop my story to. She said that after the *In Touch* interview, she had some British tabloid lined up to pay half a million dollars for my story.

I hung up and said to myself, *This cannot happen.* Mainly because I still hadn't told Glen. I would think about it in the middle of the night, but come morning I always lost my nerve. I didn't want to put any additional stress on him. I had been secretly hoping I would somehow fail the lie detector test and the whole story would go away. I'd be out the money, but fifteen thousand dollars was pennies compared to what I would be spending going forward. The only reason I was doing it was because of that "someone else" willing to tell my story.

Finally, I started easing Glen into it, doing some of the worst acting of my entire life.

"Hey, so, I met Donald Trump a long time ago," I told him one morning while our daughter was napping. Keep going, Stormy. "I had dinner with him."

"Did you fuck him?" he shot back.

"Nooooo," I said, like the idea was preposterous. "I mean, he wanted to, so there might be a way that . . . anyway." I dropped it. We were all hanging by a thread. I started doing some magical thinking and decided it was in the realm of possibility that Glen would never see an *In Touch* magazine. Yeah.

Speaking of, my "friends" at *In Touch* called again. They said they were excited about the story. "Even though you passed the lie detector test," said the editor, "we have to do due diligence and see if Mr. Trump wants to comment."

Well, that would make it real for sure. And I couldn't very well say, "Oh, God, don't do that." That wouldn't be right. I said I understood. When I hung up, I looked at my baby girl lying on the floor.

"Let's see how this goes," I said to her.

I was running late for my usual MamaFit class. I had been going religiously, twice a week, for months. It was in a complex of buildings with pre- and postnatal wellness programs. A one-stop shop for birthing ladyparts, with massage, prenatal yoga, mommy-and-me workout classes, and high-end boutiquey things. A lot of doulas and midwives kept offices there. I had found it on Facebook when I asked around for a workout class for new moms.

As I pulled in to the parking lot, I saw this guy walking around. My first thought was, *That guy is really hot. He's some-one's husband.* He was looking around, which I took to mean that he was lost in this land of ladies and moms.

I pulled into a space that would leave the passenger side open for me to get my daughter out. I always had her in the backseat on the passenger side, in a rear-facing car seat. I was in a rush, so I got out and ran around the back of the car to get to her. It was really windy, which happens in Vegas, so my hair was blow-ing in my face as I leaned into the car. My daughter dropped her toy, so I grabbed it and held it in my teeth while I fiddled with her car-seat buckle. I was basically the picture of a frustrated, harried mom.

A man came up behind me. I saw his Converse shoes first. They were navy blue and someone had drawn a star on them. Like a kid, or maybe he doodled. I turned around, taking the toy out of my teeth. It was the hot guy. He was in profile, my side to his. My eyes went up from the cool Converse, and I noticed his jeans looked expensive with a nice wash. He had both hands in his gray hoodie, which also looked expensive, with an asymmetrical zipper at the collar. His hood was down, and by the time I got to the face I was sold. He looked like a cross between Kevin Bacon, Jon Bon Jovi, and Keith Urban. A sharp, angular face like my husband Glen's, but even better built. He had a very kissable mouth. Like if you were talking to him in a bar, you would be like, "I really just want to touch your lips."

I thought he was going to ask me how to get to his wife's Lamaze class. Like, "I'm running late and all of these buildings look alike." He looked like he belonged to a woman, and nobody in three-hundred-dollar jeans asks you for a dollar. I have seen Vegas crackheads coming up to me. Not this.

"Beautiful little girl you got there," he said, leaning in to look right at my daughter.

I was readying to say, "Oh, thanks, what building are you looking for?" to save him the trouble of asking me. But he kept going.

"It'd really be a shame if something happened to her mom," he said, still looking just at her. "Forget the story. Leave Mr. Trump alone."

He walked away, and it took me a few seconds for his words

to even register. His hands stayed in his hoodie pockets. Did he want me to think he had a weapon? I looked around and he was gone. I got my daughter out of the car and I ran inside.

It wasn't until I was in the elevator that I thought, *That guy just threatened to kill me.* I stood in the center of the elevator. My face went numb and I couldn't feel my feet. I began to shake uncontrollably, and I almost dropped the baby.

I got off on the floor, got to the class, and headed straight to the bathroom. I must have looked crazy, because the instructor yelled after me, "Are you okay?"

"She had a blowout," I said, "be there in a minute." I was afraid to tell anyone. Alone in the bathroom, I held my baby close, instinctively covering her head as I stared at myself in the mirror. I was shaking still, but less now. Part of me was marveling that someone had just threatened us and dropped Mr. Trump's name.

Another part of me was just a really mad mom. That motherfucker thought that was a threat? What kind of a bad guy is that? What hit man wears sexy jeans? It just didn't make any sense to me. If he had looked at all like a threat, I wouldn't have gotten out of the car, and if I'd caught a bad vibe, I definitely would have closed my daughter's door to protect her.

"It's okay," I told my daughter. I said it again, this time to myself.

I went and did the class, telling no one what happened in the parking lot. I went back to the same coping mechanism I've always trusted: keep it moving and solve this on your own. When I left, I walked alongside people, and I scanned the lot before getting in the car. I repeatedly checked the rearview on the way home. People want to know why I didn't immediately go to the police. If you want to make a police report, it's public. This is how I imagined it would go:

"Hi, I'd like to make a report about some guy who came up and threatened me."

"Okay, what did he say?" I picture the cop as genial but by-the-book.

"He said this and this and 'leave Mr. Trump alone.'"

"Why would someone tell you to leave Mr. Trump alone?"

"Okay, it's funny. I had sex with Donald Trump and now I'm selling a story, well, someone else was trying to sell my story and I got caught up in it and I know they've reached out to Trump for comment and . . ."

Which would mean the entire world would know, including my husband. I was afraid to open a can of worms by telling Glen about the threat. Would he start to get paranoid about me leaving the house? I needed my freedom and, besides, I was used to caring for myself. Listen, if this guy had broken into my house or held me at knifepoint, I would have been like, *Fuck it, that outweighs it.* I would have gone right to the police. So, I kept it secret.

That seemed like the right decision soon enough, because *In Touch* disappeared on me. I called the girl who did the interview and she never answered the phone or returned my calls. Same with the editor. When I called Gina to see if she had heard anything, she ghosted me, too. It struck me as bizarre, because Gina was all about getting that money. I gave up contacting them, because part of me was actually relieved. Fifteen grand wasn't enough money to ruin my life.

And I hadn't told Glen. He and our daughter were my only concern. I had all the contacts that Gina had talked up as wanting to pay me crazy amounts of money once the *In Touch* story came out, but I didn't bother. None of the money seemed worth it. I let it go, content to let Donald Trump recede into the past.

EIGHT

Maybe life was too good.

By the summer of 2015, Glen and I had successfully moved our family to Texas. Glen had stopped drinking and I was transitioning out of being a porn star and becoming known more as a director. My movies are known for having stories and good dialogue, and I would often have guys coming up to me to tell me, "Thank you, your movies are the only ones my wife will watch with me." I had directed about seventy films by then and was gearing up to shoot my dream project, *Wanted*, a three-hour epic western I had been planning in my head for eight years. *Wanted* would win Best Picture and Best Director at the XBIZ Awards and Best Drama at AVN. It was the industry consensus that I was the best female director out there, and when *New York* magazine profiled me in an article titled "The Female Porn Director Winning All the Awards," I got to ask them—and by extension my colleagues—"What does my vagina have to do with directing?"

Outside my film work, I was famous enough that I provided for my family with feature dancer bookings all over the country, but not so known that I was recognized everywhere. Our daughter would soon be going to school, and not a single person in our little neighborhood knew what I did for a living.

Close to my heart, being in Texas meant I could pursue a horse career. I had a new horse I had just imported from Ireland. My horse friends don't care what I do. I had worked so hard to have the life I wanted.

Then it happened. On June 16, 2015, Donald Trump announced his presidential campaign to make America great again. Seeing Trump on TV jogged people's memories about all those times he used to call me on sets. I heard from castmates I hadn't seen in years.

"It will never happen," I would say. "He doesn't even *want* to be president."

I had a theory that he was a stalking horse for Hillary Clinton, just in the race to make it easier for her to win. It made sense, especially given what I overheard when I was at the Beverly Hills Hotel, the two friends happily discussing their plan. I didn't put it past either of them. "How does no one remember how much he has donated to her and how much he supported her last time?" I would yell at the news shows. "How are you guys missing this thing?"

As he became less of a joke candidate in the Republican primaries, people started coming out from under their rocks. Good old Gina resurfaced, acting like we had just been chatting a week before.

"You should sell your story now," she said.

"Why did you ghost me?" I flat-out asked her. "How am I supposed to trust you?"

She told me she had been threatened but didn't elaborate. She said the magazine was threatened by Trump's attorney, who she identified as Michael Cohen.

People in the industry called me, each thinking they were the first to suggest that I talk about how friendly he'd once been with a porn star. Brad Armstrong and Jessica Drake at Wicked were pressuring me to come forward because Republicans are seen as bad for the porn business. By then I no longer wanted to kill Jessica. I still didn't trust her as far as I could throw her, but we could be civil. The things that initially made her my friend were still there: she is a smart businesswoman and committed to her work. Also, once I married Glen and had a child, a fight over some man just seemed childish.

Still, when she showed up on one of my sets one day while I was in L.A., my first reaction was *What is this bitch doing here?* But that's mainly because I was directing, and I need complete control of my set.

"Hey, I need to talk to you for a sec," she said.

"Okay," I said. This was so strange that I figured it must be really important. We went over to one of the rooms I wasn't using for fucking.

"I think you need to call this person," she said, handing me Gloria Allred's card. "I'll back you up."

"No," I said.

"Just go and talk to her."

I did, but I decided against coming forward. My life was perfect. I was very happy living incognito as the most accomplished director in the business, one who could also take her daughter to playdates. And on top of that, *I still hadn't told Glen.*

Trump won Indiana on May 3, 2016. Ted Cruz and John Kasich dropped out, leaving him as the presumptive nominee. If I thought I had faced pressure before, it was nothing compared to what I got from my gay dads—well, my gay dad Keith Munyan and my *new* gay dad, JD Barrale. Keith and Dean Keefer had split, and it was like my parents getting divorced. They'd been together more than twenty years, so it was a shock. They hadn't been happy for a while, and I never saw them be affectionate or even call each other honey. While Dean and I remain close, Keith was much more of a focal point in my life.

Keith had been with his fiancé JD Barrale for about five years, and if you ask, one will say that they met in a prayer group to cue up the other.

"Yeah, the Praying-to-Get-Laid group," the other will say. They have that kind of playful relationship, and it's sweet to see Keith so happy. Still, you don't just waltz into my life. I have to haze you a little. When they first got together, I would wait until Keith left the room and I would joke, "I've got my eye on you." As I got more comfortable with JD, we would have a moment and I would say, "You know you're not my real dad. I don't have to listen to you."

I had only recently stopped hazing JD when Trump started to surge. Keith and JD each felt strongly that a Trump presidency would be a threat to them and asked me to do something about it. It was gentle nudging at first. Keith would bring him up and say a quiet, "You could stop him, you know." I always said the same thing: "I don't think his supporters would care. It's no secret he's a womanizer."

But they amped up the pressure to come forward once Trump chose Indiana governor Mike Pence as his running mate in July.

They called me on speaker from L.A. with a laundry list of things Pence had done to make life difficult for the LGBT community in Indiana.

"This shows what Trump really thinks of us," said Keith.

"Trump could do away with gay marriage," added JD.

"I don't think Trump cares if someone is gay or not," I told them. "Matter of fact, he probably hopes all the guys start fucking each other so there will be more chicks for him."

I did understand their concerns about Pence—it's kind of his thing to pick on gay people and get in their business—but Trump wouldn't care. I told them I would think about it, but the answer was still no. Besides, I was convinced Trump had no real interest in being president. He would sabotage himself without me having to ruin the lives of the people in my family, thank you.

"Are you scared now?"

My friend said it as soon as I sat down. He is a lawyer and a straight shooter, always a good resource as I make business decisions. We had arranged to meet in one of my favorite cafés in Dallas. It was three o'clock and we were the only people in there.

"Why should I be scared?" I asked. It was so hot outside—Dallas in August, no surprise—but the café had the air-conditioning on too high.

"Well, he's the Republican candidate," he said. "He's their guy now. It's not just him making decisions. And look at what politics have done to other people who knew secrets."

"What do you mean?"

He leaned forward and started reeling off names of people

who died mysteriously. Mary Meyer, Vince Foster . . . he kept going, but I didn't really recognize any names until he got to Marilyn Monroe.

"What are you trying to say?" I said. I didn't put any stock in it and rolled my eyes at him.

"Stormy," he said, "I'm not fucking around anymore. I'm completely serious." From the look on his face, I knew he was. This was one of the most sober, reasoned men I know, and he was telling me I was a target.

"If you left here right now," he continued, "and got in a 'single-car accident' or went home tonight and had an overdose . . ."

"I don't do drugs," I said.

"Doesn't matter," he said. "No matter what anyone said, there'd be a source in the paper saying, 'She hid her demons so well.' If you died tonight, no one would be like, Donald Trump or the Republicans did it. But now you're their problem. They are going to go through his closet, find his skeletons, and get rid of them. They don't want to, because they were hoping he wasn't going to get the nomination because they don't like him, either. But this is a real thing, Stormy. Think of your family. Because if a natural gas leak happens to make your house explode, there's no grieving husband on the news, either."

My daughter's face flashed in my mind, and I shook the thought away quickly. "What do you think I should do?"

"You have to come forward."

"There's that 'come forward' thing again," I said. "Why do people keep saying that? Did you all have a meeting and decide that's how to get me to do something?"

"Okay, whatever the choice of words is, the only way to keep your family safe is for your story to be out there. You want it so they can't blow up your house or cut your brake lines, because everyone would point at them and say, 'It was you!'"

When I got out and started the car, I first felt the fear that I still have every single time I turn the ignition. I wait for the boom.

I went home and started down a Google rabbit hole of political conspiracies, starting with Marilyn Monroe. If there's a mistress who died suspiciously, I read about it, and each one, no matter how far-fetched, fed my fears.

I was so serious about going public for safety reasons that at one point I was even scheduled to go on *Good Morning America*. I was in L.A. to shoot a movie when I told Keith and JD I was going to . . . dunh dunh dunh . . . "come forward." They were thrilled but got scared once I told them I was doing it for my safety. It had become my obsession. Every day this stayed secret, I felt my family was in danger. I lay awake at night. *This is gonna be bad,* I said to myself, *but if the alternative is my house blowing up . . .*

And no, I still hadn't told Glen.

On October 21, two weeks after the *Access Hollywood* "grab 'em by the pussy" tape was leaked, Jessica Drake "came forward" in a press conference with Gloria Allred. She said that while we were at the Lake Tahoe golf tournament in 2006, Trump invited her to the penthouse. Jessica stated that she didn't feel right going alone and that she went with two other women. "When we entered the room, he grabbed each of us tightly in a hug and kissed each one of us without permission." She also said that Trump invited her back to the penthouse and she was offered ten thousand dollars for sex. She said she declined, saying she had to get back to L.A., and she was offered use of his private jet. At the press conference, she was wearing a Wicked necklace, as well as glasses I had never seen on her before.

The Trump campaign responded, calling the allegation false. "Mr. Trump does not know this person, does not remember this person and would have no interest in ever knowing her." I wondered what they would say about me.

Not long after, I was on set in Malibu, directing *From This Moment*. We had just finished shooting a big rain scene when I got a call from Gina. "I need to talk to you."

"Sure."

"I need to see you in person," she said. "I can't talk on the phone."

"Well, I'm directing a movie."

"What's the address? I'll come to you."

"You can't come to set, I'm directing a movie." This is my three days a month that I'm unreachable. I call it the Bermuda Triangle. I come out and I literally don't know what day it is.

"I'm coming right now," said Gina.

"Fine," I said giving her the address. What the hell was going on? Was there a death threat against me? Did she get threatened?

She called to say she was parked at the bottom of the hill. "I can't come up because I don't want anyone to overhear us."

Okay, drama, but sure. I walked down and she had a guy with her who I had never seen before.

"What's up?" I said.

"This is Keith Davidson," she said.

I knew who he was by name, but I'd never met him. He's a Beverly Hills–based attorney who specializes in claims against celebrities, and also the lawyer who Gina supposedly had gotten to contact *The Dirty* to get the initial Trump story taken down.

I later learned that Trump's people had contacted Davidson after learning of the plan to go on *Good Morning America*. It was Trump's counsel, Michael Cohen, who reached out to him, he said, offering me $130,000 to *not* tell my story.

I felt like this was a "win." I got to stay in my home with my daughter and do the work that I love. I won't be defined by Donald fucking Trump, and I won't be branded a gold digger.

And they can't murder me. *And I don't have to tell Glen!*

Keith handed me a seventeen-page nondisclosure agreement and they opened the trunk so I could sign it right there under the light. I had no idea how they had arrived at that price for my silence, and I was too concerned about my safety to even think of wondering why Davidson didn't push for more. This wasn't about me being greedy, because if it was I would have sold the story for a million dollars three times already. This was about putting all this behind me confidentially and never having to worry about Trump coming after me or my family.

I just had to break it to Keith and JD that I wasn't going to talk after all. They were disappointed but seemed to understand.

In the meantime, I went back home to where I live in Texas and I waited for the money. It said in the contract they had seven days to wire me the money, so every day I would check my balance, wondering if that was the day I'd get paid. And on the seventh day, I freaked out.

I knew just what a creep Donald Trump is. He would wait until after the election and then just not pay me. If he lost, nobody would care that he had sex with me. If he won, he'd be the president of the United States and could drop a nuclear bomb on me if he wanted.

They later sent me a new contract because the first one had been breached for their failure to pay, but I was alone in Texas. I took it to the notary near my house. If there weren't already enough problems, the notary stamped it but didn't sign or date it. She also notarized a blank signature line.

Ten days before the election, Cohen wired the $130,000 to Davidson, who then took out his and Gina's share. He then wired the balance of eighty grand and change to Glen's account, not mine, so if anybody looked at my bank records there would be no red flags.

And I finally told Glen. Well, I told him some of it.

"Look, I am getting this money from Donald Trump because I was in a hotel with him," I said. "Nothing happened, but his wife would get mad, and having dinner with a porn star would look bad."

He believed me. I had never lied to him before, so it didn't occur to him to question it. He trusted me, and I have to live with that. He also believed me because eighty thousand dollars is just such a perfect amount, a ludicrous number for what really happened. People can say I am a gold digger and a liar, but I signed something giving me a paltry amount when I could have made millions of dollars. I am not that stupid. I just wanted it to stop. I used the money to buy a new horse trailer, and I thought that was the end of it.

Four days before the election, *The Wall Street Journal* ran a story about the *National Enquirer* paying former Playmate Karen McDougal $150,000 to tell her story about an affair with Trump, and then not running it. She'd had a ten-month relationship with Trump starting in 2006, the same year I met him. Welcome to the shitty club, sister. Her description of their "dates" sounds a lot like mine—a meet-up in Lake Tahoe, beauty pageants, and those damn steaks at the Beverly Hills Hotel. Except the poor thing had sex with him multiple times. Karen said that when she turned down his offer of money after their first encounter, he told her, "You are special."

The *WSJ* reporters quoted sources who said the *National Enquirer* did a "catch and kill," where they buy the story but bury it so it stays secret. David Pecker, the CEO and chairman of *National Enquirer* publisher American Media, Inc., has called Trump "a personal friend." Later, *The New Yorker*'s Ronan Farrow would get McDougal on the record talking about what a terrible deal she got. The *National Enquirer* had her locked down so that if she breathed a word about Trump to anyone, she would be sued for $150,000 in damages.

And guess who her lawyer was on this terrible deal? Say it with me: Keith Davidson. According to her account in *The New Yorker*, McDougal had a friend, John Crawford, who suggested she talk, and she gave him permission to pursue it after someone started blabbing about it on social media. Like me, she didn't want someone else profiting off her story and getting the facts wrong. Crawford called someone involved in the adult film industry—let's go with the alias Deep Throat—who then called Davidson. *The New Yorker* published excerpts of an August 2016 email exchange that sounded a lot like my interactions with Davidson. When McDougal asked about some of the fine print, he encouraged her to just sign the deal. "If you deny, you are safe" was his reply. "We really do need to get this signed and wrapped up. . . ."

By the way, according to *The New Yorker*, Karen also got screwed when Crawford, Deep Throat, and Davidson each took their cut, dropping her check by 45 percent. She walked away with just $82,500.

I didn't vote on Election Day because I couldn't decide between Clinton and Trump. So, if you think I am some sort of Deep State Clinton operative, I am sorry to disappoint you.

And then the motherfucker won.

That night, when Trump won, my gay dads lost their shit on me.

"How could you do this to us?" JD texted me. "You could have stopped him."

I disagreed and I stand by it. This is a guy who bragged on tape about assaulting women. Me saying I slept with him would just be another consensual notch on his belt that his fans could pat him on the back about. Look what happened to Karen McDougal: everyone knew she had sex with him and it didn't make one bit of difference except, well, now everyone knows she had sex with him.

JD was scared that night. He said they were probably not going to be able to get married. "You don't love us," he said. Keith, a man who I hadn't had a single disagreement with in twenty years, chimed in. "You're dead to us. Don't ever talk to us again."

That's when I started crying. Keith's words gutted me. They are family to me—and now I truly felt disowned. I put the phone down. I knew they were wrong, but still, some part of me felt I had failed them. I was so afraid of my family paying a price for me talking, and now I'd lost them because of my silence.

NINE

For a whole year, everything was calm. Well, as calm as my life ever is. I remember 2017 as pretty damn magical. I had been so stressed about all the Trump stuff that I was able to appreciate the weight being lifted. There is a specific moment I remember from Christmas Eve: We were at home, all of us in our pajamas. My daughter and I made cookies and she left them out for Santa. As I write this, she is still that perfect age of seven, when you are so freaking smart, but you still believe in things. She was so excited, and I looked at Glen.

"What?" he asked.

"I'm happy," I said, embarrassed at being so cheesy. "Fuck off, I'm happy."

We all were. Even my gay dads JD and Keith came around. We agreed Election Night was tough, but we were going to leave it behind us.

Then, on January 9, 2018, I got a text from Gina. "There's some rumblings. Don't say anything."

I hadn't heard from her in an entire year. It was strange, but I figured nothing would come of it. I certainly wasn't going to say anything. The following morning, I got a call from Keith

Davidson. I was not going to talk to him, but he sounded weird in his voice mail.

I later learned that Michael Cohen had called and wanted a statement signed because he claimed the press was all over the story.

I read it and it was pretty soft. It began, "I recently became aware that certain news outlets are alleging that I had a sexual and/or romantic affair with Donald Trump many, many, many years ago." Well, I wouldn't call what we had an affair, but I guess that's not a lie. But I didn't see any news outlets saying anything. In fact, I was so panicked about a story being out there that I immediately googled every variation of my name and Trump's that I could think of, scouring the internet and coming up with nothing. What was Cohen even talking about?

The end of the statement was actually kind of cheeky and sounded like me. "If indeed I did have a relationship with Donald Trump," it read, "trust me, you wouldn't be reading about it in the news, you would be reading about it in my book."

I signed it, sent it back. And nothing happened. I had no idea that it was one of my last days of true freedom.

The morning of Friday, January 12, I boarded a plane for New Jersey to talk about a potential movie. Around three that afternoon, all hell broke loose. *The Wall Street Journal*'s Michael Rothfeld and Joe Palazzolo, the same reporters who broke Karen McDougal's story, posted an article headlined TRUMP LAWYER ARRANGED $130,000 PAYMENT FOR ADULT-FILM STAR'S SILENCE. There was a huge picture of me and Trump from the golf tournament. Throughout, they refer to me as Stephanie Clifford—

only the IRS calls me that—and refer to sources as "people familiar with the matter."

They contacted Michael Cohen, who just happened to have the January 10 statement Davidson made me sign saying nothing happened. But it just made me look like a liar, and I couldn't defend myself at all.

I was trapped. The press was outside my hotel and people were randomly knocking on my door. It was really warm for Jersey in January, sixty degrees and sunny, so people didn't mind camping out waiting for me. I turned on the TV and everything was "porn star Stormy Daniels" and "pornographic actor Stormy Daniels."

I called Glen. "Stormy, what the hell is going on?" People had pounded on our front door asking him if his wife slept with Donald Trump. He didn't know what the hell they were talking about, so he turned on the news and there's everyone talking about his wife having sex with the president.

"It's not really true," I said. "I gave a statement saying it's not true." I worried about our daughter. "You cannot have any TV on. It's all over."

"Jesus, Stormy," he said.

I wanted to be home, I wanted to be anywhere but where I was, trapped in a New Jersey hotel with everyone wanting a picture or comment from the porn star. I was alone—no roadie, no assistant, certainly no bodyguard. I got 472 unique text messages the first day and just hid in the hotel. I just hid out for forty-eight hours with no food until a friend finally brought me Chinese food. We sat there in the hotel, eating sweet and sour chicken with brown rice and some awful dumplings. We watched TV until I just had to turn it off.

But my phone kept buzzing. Not one of those 472 messages was from Wicked. How is it that someone could text me, "Hey I curled your hair in 2006, remember me?" but not the people I'd made so much money for? Not even a "What do you want us to say? Our phone is blowing up." Much less, "How are you? Is there anything you need? How is your family?" Nothing. Keiran Lee from Brazzers, an adult film production company, reached out. I am friends with his wife, Kirsten Price. He told me if I ever left Wicked I would have a home at Brazzers.

Finally, I was able to get home. Glen had a basket of business cards reporters had put under the door when he stopped answering. There was no way I was going to talk.

It got so much worse the next day, when *In Touch* published my 2011 interview as a cover story. The story had so many details, and it was unmistakably my voice—I could no longer lie to Glen.

We were in our living room at home after our daughter was in bed.

"Yes, it happened," I told him. "Once. And it was before we met."

"It doesn't matter," he said. "I found out from some fucker knocking on my door. And then *you* lied to me. Everyone knew but me!"

"I know," I said. "I know. But it felt like too much time had passed and I just couldn't tell you."

"Is there anything else I need to know?" he screamed. "Why didn't you trust me?"

"I was doing the best I could. I was trying to keep us safe."

"I could have handled it."

"No, you couldn't," I said. "You have no idea how hard this has been. I was so worried about you."

He said something cruel, which I probably felt like I deserved. I stormed off to our bedroom and closed the door. I waited for him to come in that night, but he didn't. He spent the night on the couch, where he began to spend pretty much every night. It just became our pattern. Just another change.

To protect our daughter, our TV hasn't been on for months, unless it's a DVD or the Disney Channel. We can't turn on the radio in our car. She knows that I write, direct, and star in movies, but she is too young to know what sex is. I never lie to her, so what she knows is that her mom makes movies that are just for adults, in the way that there are action and horror films that kids can't watch. When she's older and we have the sex talk, the very next conversation will be about my work. Trust me, I am far more worried about her reaction to finding out about Santa Claus than about my career.

But I don't want her finding out from other people. She was set to start a new school in January, but we decided for her safety that we needed to homeschool her. We have a tutor for her now, which is crazy expensive, but I want to make sure she is getting the education she deserves. A first grader, she is already reading at a second-grade level, and she is spot on for math for first grade. And forget history, science, and social skills—she is off the charts. I'm so relieved I am not slowing her down, but there are other costs. Glen took our daughter out for pancakes and a man approached them and told them that her mother is nothing but a whore. I stopped going to Starbucks because the press figured out my routine.

"Hi, Stormy, can we talk for a just a minute?"

"Stormy, is there anything you want to say?"

Our daughter knows who Donald Trump is because he's the president. We were being followed, and enough people kept approaching me that she wanted to know what was going on. We were in bed, and she was nestled against me, this sweet girl who's so cool she knows every word to Drowning Pool's "Bodies" but still wants to cuddle. I decided to level with her, giving her information appropriate to her age.

"Donald Trump did something bad a long time ago when Mommy used to know him," I said. "People know that *I* know what he did. And they want to talk to me and get answers about it."

"Okay," she said. I smoothed her hair and looked up. Everything that I had tried to keep from happening—and turned down millions of dollars to keep from happening—was happening. And I couldn't even stand up for myself because of the NDA. I had to just take it. *We* just had to take it.

On the morning of January 20, I got yet another call from Keith Davidson. They wanted me to sign another statement but I refused. Because I was fine with saying nothing, but I'm not okay with lying.

I had lied enough. My husband wasn't speaking to me, he was sleeping on the couch, saying he couldn't trust me anymore. Everything was going great—this is craziness. I just wanted it to go away.

I hadn't said a word, and these people kept coming back again and again. I would not lie for these people. Your integrity is all you have. Money comes and goes, but if you don't have your word, no one will stand with you when you need them.

That night I was heading to South Carolina for a dance booking at the Trophy Club in Greenville. Jay Levy, the club owner, had advertised it as the first stop on my Make America Horny Again tour. He had made flyers of the golf tournament photo. "HE SAW HER LIVE!" it read. "YOU CAN TOO!" A lot of the subsequent clubs I was booked at followed suit with the Make America Horny Again name, which he also trademarked. I hated the name and thought it was tacky, mainly because I don't like the appearance that I'm piggybacking off someone else's idea. I know now that everyone assumed it was my idea and that I was profiting off the Trump scandal I wasn't supposed to be talking about.

Driving up to the club, I saw there was a news truck parked outside. I was so unprepared, because it's a great club that I've been to several times. I didn't even bring an assistant with me. *The New York Times, The Washington Post, TMZ*—all there to jot down notes while I did my two shows that night, 11 P.M. and 1 A.M. They asked me questions, and I completely understand they had a job to do. I just felt ridiculous not being able to answer basic questions.

While I was at the club, *Saturday Night Live* spoofed "me" on Weekend Update. It was up on YouTube quick, so I watched it the next morning, scared to death. I was terrified because *SNL* is my favorite show, bar none. I have a crush on Colin Jost and I would have been so sad if he made fun of me. Random Instagram trolls saying "Die slut"—I mean, whatever, but if Colin said something mean? Don't go breaking my heart. Fortunately, he didn't. Cecily Strong did the impersonation of me. Her boobs looked good and I giggled, so good for her.

The Monday after *SNL* spoofed me, I got scared when I saw a news story about Common Cause, a nonprofit watchdog group, filing a federal complaint with the Federal Election Commission charging Trump with violating campaign finance laws when he made the $130,000 payment to me eleven days before the election. "The funds were paid for the purpose of influencing the 2016 presidential general election," they wrote in a letter to Attorney General Jeff Sessions. Basically, if it was a contribution to the campaign, it needed to be reported to the FEC. Of course, it wasn't.

TEN

The Marilyn Monroe suite at the Roosevelt Hotel is one of the most beautiful places to stay in Hollywood. The soft light glints off the white leather of the furniture and the tan wood of the walls, and there are mirrors everywhere—including on the ceiling over the bed—so you can constantly catch yourself doing a Marilyn pose. Her ghost is supposed to still be hanging out there, too. We would have a lot to talk about.

The very nice people at *Jimmy Kimmel Live* thought it was funny to put me up there for my January 30 appearance on the show. I was scheduled to go on live after Trump's second State of the Union address. I got in late in the afternoon, and I had invited some friends over, because what good is staying in the freaking Marilyn Monroe suite if you can't share it?

Gina had called, saying she had clothes for me to wear that night on *Kimmel,* and also for *The View,* which she had scheduled me on for later that week in New York. What's funny is that once you're famous, people just want to give you free shit. Tonia Ryan had made me the most beautiful dress I have ever worn for the January 27 AVN Awards. It was electric blue and elegant, and made Thunder and Lightning look amazing. Of course, I was excited to get more from her.

My friends were all stuck in traffic, so I was alone when Gina came by with the dress. When she came into the suite, she walked in with a bearded man in a Gucci shirt who I later found out was her boyfriend. And Keith Davidson.

I gave Gina a look, and she knew exactly what I was thinking. "Oh, we just want to talk about possible answers for you to give Jimmy," she said.

Got it. Media training. Nothing odd about that. Right?

Gina distracted me with literally something shiny—a gorgeous dress in a similar color to the AVN one, but lacy and shorter. And then we sat down at the glass table in the Marilyn suite to talk about what I could say. Gucci guy, who I didn't know at all, sat next to me. I then learned that Cohen had once again reached out to Davidson.

It made me uneasy that Michael Cohen and Keith Davidson always seemed to be talking.

I was then given yet another statement to sign. I sat up to read it. "The fact of the matter is that each party to this alleged affair denied its existence in 2006, 2011, 2016, 2017, and now again in 2018," the signed statement read. "I am not denying this affair because I was paid 'hush money' as has been reported in overseas-owned tabloids. I am denying this affair because it never happened."

I panicked. I admit it, I panicked. I didn't know who the Gucci guy was. Was he the one threatening me? Did he have a gun? Even though I knew the statement was complete bullshit, I picked up the pen and signed my name.

But I purposely signed it wrong. "Stormy Daniels" has a very distinct signature. I have signed my boobs on magazine covers for many years. I signed the statement like it was my first day as a grown-up, girly and bubby. I wanted to signal there was something amiss here.

My girlfriends showed up. I didn't say a word to them, and if I seemed shaken to them, they probably thought I was uncharacteristically nervous about going on live TV. In no time, Michael Cohen had the statement, and he released it three hours before the show. Thanks, Keith Davidson. Always advocating for his clients, that guy.

Jimmy had a printout of the statement at his desk, and with no tip-off whatsoever from me, he brought up the signature right away on the air.

"This is what fascinates me," he said. "The signature on your original statement does not match the signature on this statement." He pulled out a bunch of signed photos he'd found on the internet as examples of my real signature. "Am I getting at anything? Did you sign this letter that was released today?"

"I don't know, did I?" I said. "That does *not* look like my signature, does it?"

I was scared to say too much, so I ended up looking like a complete idiot. I couldn't answer the most basic questions. He had this bit planned where he gave me a Stormy Muppet so I could talk to his Donald Trump Muppet. Jimmy was amazing, and such a class act, but I couldn't help him. I felt my hands were tied.

Everyone thinks I'm a buffoon, I thought. Jimmy was so understanding and kind. He could tell I'd been railroaded. He took me aside afterward and told me that when I was ready to speak, he could devote the whole show to it. We could change the whole format, even pretaping it and allowing me to see it so I felt more comfortable. "Just tell me when you're ready," he said. He also donated to my legal fund and urged others to do the same. It was so odd to have someone genuinely looking out for me, offering to help. He has privately checked in on me, and later, he went on his show to ask viewers to join him in donating to my legal fund. "I never thought giving money to a porn star would be considered an act of patriotism," he told his audience, "but then again I never thought a guy who got into a Twitter war with Cher would become president."

That night I went back to my suite and canceled the appearance on *The View*. It would just be more of me sitting dumbly—humiliated and unable to stand up for myself. Because I wasn't able to say anything, people could come to their own conclusions and put whatever motives or labels they wanted on me. The Republican Trump fans, weirdly, thought I was great because I was obviously lying to protect the president. The liberals could just write me off as a set of tits with no brain. I could do nothing. My husband was on the couch, my kid couldn't watch TV, and America—no actually, the whole world—thought I was at worst a liar and at best an idiot.

In the bed, I looked up at the mirror on the ceiling, sighed, and went into a sexy pose to make myself laugh. "Hey, Marilyn," I said to the empty room. "Feel free to jump in anytime with some advice."

I had a few days off around Valentine's Day, so I went home to Texas to be with Glen and our daughter. I'd put in a ten-thousand-dollar alarm system to be safe, but this was before I realized that any time paparazzi saw a gap in my schedule, they figured it was worth camping out to get shots of "porn star Stormy Daniels" and her family. The morning of February 13, I was up early sipping coffee in my mug with Elsa from *Frozen* on it, just checking my messages to see who was calling me a whore that day. You know, just a working mom starting her day.

I nearly spit out my coffee when I saw the *Daily Beast* head-line: TRUMP'S LAWYER MICHAEL COHEN IS SHOPPING A BOOK ABOUT THE FIRST FAMILY, STORMY DANIELS, AND RUSSIA. This fool had the nerve to draw up an NDA saying that Trump and I were supposed to forget each other existed, and now he was pitching publishers using my goddamn name? In his book pro-posal, with the shitty title *Trump Revolution: From The Tower to The White House, Understanding Donald J. Trump*, Cohen promised to tell all about his role as a fixer for the family. "No issue was too big, too sticky or too oddball for me to tackle," Cohen wrote in the proposal, which the *Daily Beast* said it obtained after it was sent to multiple publishers for consider-ation. "I saw it all, handled it all. And still do." The article said Cohen promised to clarify his role in the "unfortunate saga" involving me.

And even the proposal had a threat. "There truly is a method to his madness, to quote that old saw, and people who think otherwise can quickly get buried," Cohen said. "Steve Bannon comes to mind, but there are plenty of others who are now six feet under due to this basic miscalculation."

Cohen confirmed the contents of the proposal, telling the *Daily Beast*, "I have been working on a book and am extremely thankful that it has been well received and sought after by mul-tiple publishers."

This dim bulb Cohen was out there selling a book on my name, but I was the only person taking this NDA seriously? I can't comment, profit, or defend myself?

Right on the heels of that, Cohen announced that he had paid me the $130,000 out of his own pocket. "In a private transaction in 2016, I used my own personal funds to facilitate a payment of $130,000 to Ms. Stephanie Clifford," he said in a statement to *The New York Times*. "Neither the Trump Organization nor the Trump campaign was a party to the transaction with Ms. Clifford, and neither reimbursed me for the payment, either directly or indirectly. The payment to Ms. Clifford was lawful, and was not a campaign contribution or a campaign expenditure by anyone." He concluded, "Just because something isn't true doesn't mean that it can't cause you harm or damage. I will always protect Mr. Trump."

It was a big day for Cohen flapping his gums. Could he really do this and not invalidate the NDA? I got out the contract and read it again. The last time I'd looked at the NDA was when I signed it in the trunk of a car.

I read every word, including one set of sentences in the second paragraph. It specifically says, "It is an essential element of this Settlement Agreement that the Parties"—Trump and me—"shall never directly or indirectly communicate with each other or attempt to contact their respective families." "Directly" means I can't call Trump or Melania and say, "Hey, whatcha wearing?" And he can't do the same to me or Glen, thank God.

But indirectly? Michael Cohen reached out to me multiple times. There were the two times when he got Davidson to ask me to sign statements, and the one time I initially refused. Then he was shopping a book proposal using my name as a draw, and now he was volunteering to *The New York Times* that he paid me himself.

All this time, I upheld my end of the contract that I had signed without any negotiation and that I thought Trump had signed as well. I was done being bullied and done being the only one doing what I said I was going to do. I decided they couldn't intimidate me any longer. I took it and took it again because I thought I was doing the right thing. But what if I was just doing the dumb thing and getting screwed?

They'd repeatedly breached the contract. And I was skeptical about Keith Davidson. I was worried that he and Michael Cohen seemed so chummy. And at the very least, he was a fucking pussy who was incapable of advocating for his client. As a lawyer, if someone approaches you and says, "We want your client to do this," you either say, "No," or you say, "What's in it for my client?" If Michael Cohen kept wanting me to sign more shit, he should have offered me more money. I'm not saying I would have taken it. I'm saying it was never even put on the table or raised as a possibility by Davidson. Also, Davidson would get a huge cut of anything I got. It was a red flag that he never brought any asks to Cohen. But I was afraid to go to another lawyer.

Sure enough, after I approached Davidson with my view that the contract had been breached, he reacted exactly as I suspected he would. He did nothing.

The next day, first thing in the morning Valentine's Day, Gina gave the story to *The Blast*, an online celebrity news site. The AP got wind of it and published a story with the headline PORN STAR

WHO ALLEGED TRUMP AFFAIR: I CAN NOW TELL MY STORY. For me, it was a declaration that I was done getting screwed every which way but well. For Gina, it was maybe an advertisement that my story was up for sale. Gina had all these offers from people, hundreds of thousands of dollars in play, from TV movies to several reality series options. Separately, my assistant Kayla was using several of her connections to broker a reality show deal that would have been incredibly lucrative for me—and yes, for her. They were focused on instant gratification and a lot of money, and I'm not faulting them. In their defense, this looked like a single-news-cycle story. They had no idea the story would become so much bigger than just a payout, with talk of corruption and cover-ups.

I didn't tell them that I had started to think that I was tired of not being taken seriously. If I went with Jimmy Kimmel and did the show for free, then it would show people I wasn't a gold digger. I had a job, and you know I've never dated any rich dudes. The American Academy of Gold Diggers would not think much of my membership application. "So let's see, the guy she moved in with when she was seventeen had a mattress and a couple of CD shelves on the floor," I can imagine a panel judge saying. "And when she moved in with her husband, who it says here she married for—how quaint—love, he had a mattress . . . and a skateboard."

If I'm a gold digger, I'm fucking stupid as shit.

That said, I knew how much a money windfall would change the lives of my friends and family. I felt awful. They had the opportunity to make a lot of money, but I decided they couldn't because of my morals. I know how it looked: What a pretentious bitch. Me on my pornographic high horse over here.

Now, I just needed a decent lawyer to help me tell my story and really advocate for me. I spoke with one who seemed to take the call just for the curiosity factor. He was a very high-powered lawyer, but I just wasn't getting the sense that he understood what a big deal this was. He dragged it out for a couple of weeks and was moving so slow, I knew he didn't share my passion, so I ended it. I was anxious that this guy now knew my story and my strategy for confronting Cohen and Trump. After my experience with Davidson, I didn't exactly trust lawyers.

The next guy was 100 percent on my side and Mr. Gung Ho. "Oh, yeah," he said, incredulous about what hapless lawyers Davidson and Cohen were. "You totally have a case here."

"Great, let's do this," I said. He was based in L.A., another high-powered lawyer, and we talked on the phone a few more times. It seemed to be going well, so I felt safe sending him a copy of the NDA I signed. We arranged to meet at his office when I was in L.A. for a photo shoot on February 26. I had decided to leave Wicked Pictures after seventeen years and take Keiran Lee up on his offer to make a home at Digital Playground.

Literally two hours before our appointment, when I was finally set to meet him in person, he called to cancel. "I can't meet you today," he said.

"You're kidding," I said. What was wrong with lawyers? Can't a girl just take on the most powerful man in the world with a decent lawyer at her side?

"I need you to meet an associate of mine," he said. "I think he would be a better fit for your case. Where's your shoot at?"

I told him and he paused. "Oh, a good place to meet is the bar at the Waldorf Astoria in Beverly Hills," he said. "The lounge in the lobby. He likes it there."

"Okay," I said, not trying to hide that I was pissed I was being dumped onto some guy who was probably a junior attorney. "What's this guy's name?"

"Michael," he said. "Michael Avenatti."

ELEVEN

You know when you look good? I looked good. I went straight from the photo shoot to the Waldorf Astoria in Beverly Hills. I brought my assistant Kayla with me, since I wasn't sure there wasn't something fishy going on. Kayla is beautiful, with brown hair and a small streak of lovable crazy. I was angry when I walked in, because I had gone through all these lawyers, and every person I told was another potential leak.

We entered the lobby lounge and stood at the edge. The hotel had just opened the summer before and was done up in a 1920s art deco style, with lots of sleek Gatsby touches like a crystal waterfall chandelier and an ornate fireplace. A man in a suit was standing at the fireplace, his back to us as he sipped a martini.

"That's probably him," I said.

He turned his head toward us in a classic leading man move, but he did a double take. Neither of us expected the other to look so good. We had, as they say, a moment.

"Oh, my God, he's so fucking hot," Kayla said.

"Be cool," I said. Let's just say it: he is gorgeous. He walked right over to us with his hand out, super charming.

"You must be—"

"Stormy," I said, extending my hand.

He took it, looking right at me with these ridiculous blue eyes. "Michael Avenatti," he said.

I jostled Kayla to stop her from staring. "This is my assistant."

He gestured to a small table with three chairs, and we sat. He ordered another martini, and he did it so suavely that it felt wrong not to get a cocktail, so I went with a vodka cranberry. I would need something to distract me if I had to go through the whole saga and watch my assistant try to eye-fuck this lawyer.

"So," he said, "tell me what happened."

I was still mad about being stood up by the other lawyer and saddled with this pretty boy. I barreled through it, telling the whole story brashly because this was going to be one more guy who just wanted to hear about the freak show but wouldn't actually do anything to help me. I could tell this Avenatti was sizing me up and down, trying to figure out if I was lying or not.

I'm colorful when I speak, and I don't hold a lot back. I didn't talk to Avenatti any differently from how I talk to Kayla, or Keith, or anybody else I know.

I saw a crack in his façade as he smiled. Michael now says that's the moment he fell in love with me as a client. The moment he realized I owned who I was and wasn't afraid to acknowledge it.

I looked Michael up on Wikipedia that night. "He's forty-seven," I told Kayla. "Race car driver on the side." I saved the photo of him for the caller ID on my phone. I reeled off a bunch of his cases, and Kayla just looked at me like I was speaking dolphin.

"Single?" she asked.

"Separated."

"Hmmph," said Kayla.

"I'm not taking on the president to get you laid," I said.

"Yeah, but if it was an added benefit . . ." she said.

Since I got to choose where we were going, I thought I'd haze him a little. I told Mr. Waldorf Astoria boy to meet me at an out-of-the-way dive bar I know on Sunset and Hollywood. Kayla, of course, wanted to come along, still desperate to fuck him.

Kayla and I ordered the fish tacos, and Michael said he wasn't hungry. Getting down to his fighting weight, I guess. And there, in the dive bar, we worked out our strategy.

TWELVE

Back home in Texas, I assigned Michael a specific ringtone so I would know to slip into another room to talk if I was with people, especially my daughter. It was the Bat Signal, and Batgirl here was busy. Michael had called Andy Court, the *60 Minutes* producer he had worked with on a story about his lawsuit against medical giant Kimberly-Clark Corporation and its tech firm spin-off Halyard Health. Michael proved they were misleading buyers about the safety of surgical gowns sold during the Ebola crisis. Michael was really proud of winning the case, and if Michael is proud of something, you're gonna hear about it. The gowns were more porous than the company told people, consistently failing industry standards. After the piece aired, an L.A. jury found Kimberly-Clark and Halyard Health liable for fraud and awarded $454 million in damages.

So Michael vouching for my credibility had some weight at *60 Minutes*, but hey, I'm still a porn star. Producer Andy Court and associate producer Evie Salomon had a lot of initial questions they wanted Michael to relay to me. Then, when they brought the potential story to executive producer Jeff Fager, he wanted additional fact-checking before they committed to even investigating the story.

I was impressed that they took it so seriously. I wasn't offended, mostly because I found it amusing that Michael seemed ever so slightly put off that his assurance, "Guys, she's cool," wasn't enough to get me through the door. So I pulled out my feature dancing calendar for March to see where I could squeeze in *60 Minutes* coming to my house in Texas. I wanted Glen there, at least in the beginning of the meeting, because it was important to me that he feel included after I hid so much from him. I was leaving town for a two-night dance booking in Houston on March 2, so I offered March 1.

Michael got to the house an hour before the producers and met Glen for the first time.

I had arranged for my daughter to play at a neighbor's house during the meeting. She could meet the TV people, but she had to be gone quickly so we could talk. As she did cartwheels in the living room, the car pulled up and Michael opened the door for Andy and Evie. He was a little older, she seemed young and very serious. Glen left after saying a quick hello, making it clear he was not going to be interviewed and wanted no part of any of this.

"I'll see you later," I said.

"Yeah," he said, shaking his head as he left.

Normally, if someone came into my home, I would offer a drink. You know I love snacks, and yeah, sometimes I put them out more for me than for the guests, but I at least offer them. But in this situation, they could have a bottle of water and that was it. I didn't want any appearance that I was trying to influence them or for their opinion to be based on anything other than facts. I wanted to present what I would present on a television interview: the facts. Because I think that's good enough. I felt about the producers how I felt about the *60 Minutes* viewers. I don't need anyone to like me or to try and change anyone's opinion of me as a woman or a performer or a slut or a whore. Yes, I wish people would think that porn stars are people, but that wasn't my agenda for this. These producers could sit in my living room and think I'm a disgusting human being and I deserve to burn in hell, but I wanted them to have to follow that up with "But she never called the president and blackmailed him. She came forward because they called her and wanted her to lie. Her reasoning for the decisions she made is clear."

I told them the whole story, not wasting a second trying to be charming. They kept asking follow-up questions, sometimes trying to catch me by asking the same question in a different way. It felt like an interrogation, and I just told the truth. My daughter would pop back in every now and again, and we would all stop talking until she left again. They were the first people to hear just about everything, and every once in a while, their stoic faces would crack, unable to avoid a look at each other of *This is big.*

Michael loved those moments, and every single time, he said, "I told you guys."

We talked for so long, they almost missed their flight back to New York. They left in a sort of daze, sponges that needed to be wrung out.

That night I went to Houston for my weekend dance booking at Vivid club. On March 3, I met Denver Nicks, who wanted to profile me for *Rolling Stone*. He had reached out to me on Twitter and I loved his energy. He's this brilliant guy from Oklahoma who has impeccable grammar and a deep voice that makes everything he says sound important. He got me right away, and I didn't think of the story as a potential conflict with *60 Minutes,* since I assumed the episode would come out before the magazine did. While I was in Houston, Michael called me with an update. The producers must have thought it went well.

We settled on a time later in the month when I had a day free and even asked my makeup artist to hold the date. On March 6, Michael filed suit against President Trump on my behalf, alleging that he had purposefully left his signature off the NDA so he could later "publicly disavow any knowledge of the Hush Agreement and Ms. Clifford." If Trump—or "David Dennison"—didn't sign it, the agreement was null and void. I was under no obligation to keep anything confidential.

Maybe the filing got *60 Minutes* ticking faster. The morning of March 7, we settled on the next day for the interview in Myrtle Beach, where I had a show.

I looked through my closet, settling on a black pencil skirt and red blouse to keep Thunder and Lightning in check. I didn't have time to get my makeup artist, because originally I was supposed to go to New York, and Michael assured me they could bring one. They had scouted a hotel with villas where we wouldn't be recognized and set a call time for 6 A.M.

The night before, I did my 10 P.M. and 1 A.M. shows at Thee DollHouse. With the meet-and-greet after, I didn't get back to my hotel until four in the morning. I had two hours before I needed to be at the other hotel for the interview.

I was still wired from the show but tried to sleep. My assistant Kayla was out like a light, and I left her at the hotel when

Michael sent the car service for me. The crew was extremely rushed when I got there. The lighting crew was local, and they were trying to set up and sign NDAs at the same time.

A makeshift makeup room in the cramped office bathroom had been set up. I pushed open the door, right into Anderson Cooper.

"I never thought we'd be having our first meeting in a men's room," I said.

He laughed. He was just finishing up getting his makeup done. When he came out he shook my hand and said he was looking forward to it. I took his spot in the makeup chair.

The makeup woman seemed nervous and rushed, and for one brief second I considered telling her I would just do my makeup myself. But I was so tired I thought, *Oh, fuck it,* and let her do it. I should have just slept in my makeup from the night before, but that probably would have been too much. A little dramatic and strippery. Though now I would take full Raging Whore over what I got.

It's not really her fault. She started my makeup and the whole time, they were knocking on the door, asking "How much longer?" so she was super panicked.

Finally, I was seated across from Anderson. I was calm, ready to tell the truth.

"I think some people listening to this," he said as the cameras rolled, "are going to think that you're an opportunist. That you're just trying to get the most money you can. This is an opportunity for you and you're just trying to grab the money while you can."

"Which is exactly why I'm sitting here," I said. "Not getting paid."

"We're not paying you."

"Correct." *Sigh,* I thought.

"We didn't get you a hotel room. We haven't flown you here."

"No." About four hours before, I was picking up dollars at a strip club that brought me here, dude.

I had prepped by watching some of his interviews on YouTube, just to see if he had a "gotcha" trick thing he would do before he tries to throw you. I didn't see any, and I don't think he has one. He seemed genuine and eager to just let me talk. The interview was three hours, and I *still* didn't say everything I wanted to say. It was so long that I wondered how they could possibly edit it down to, what, eighteen minutes?

Afterward, I asked Anderson if I could take a picture with him. "I know this is secret and I won't show anybody, but when the story is out I really want to show it to my dads."

"Your dads?" he said.

"Yeah, they're gay and they're big fans of yours," I said. "I know I can't get an autograph or anything because it's proof we met."

"Well, I can autograph a book and send it to them once this is out." I gave him their address and names and didn't think that he would follow through. (He did!)

I was under the impression that they were going to rush it on the air that Sunday. They kept pushing it because they needed to verify my story and fact-check, and I started to get annoyed, feeling that they were flat-out calling me a liar when I knew every word I said was true. They freaked out when *Rolling Stone* posted Denver's story on me on March 9, earlier than I thought it would. I thought it was the best thing anyone had ever written about me, so I wasn't apologetic about it. Plus, Denver had become a close friend, someone I could actually trust. Through Michael, *60 Minutes* demanded to know what other interviews I had done.

Meanwhile, as they waited, I was catching all sorts of shit and couldn't fully defend myself. I tried to relieve the pressure by batting at some of the trolls who came at me on Twitter. When someone tweeted asking if I was worried I was going to go to hell from taking so many dicks, I had some fun. "Does heaven have a maximum dick-taking number? More importantly, does hell have a minimum? Just want to make sure my quota is on track."

"Pretty sure dumb whores go to hell," some guy named Scott wrote.

"Glad I'm a smart one," I answered.

A woman's response blew my mind. "A very smart one," a girl named Stephanie wrote. "I wish every woman had the confidence you do and the ability to not take personally people's lame insults. Whether you're an adult film star or a teacher or whatever, if you're a woman, you'll be called a whore one day. Let's not let that lame insult affect us."

I blinked a few times, rereading the tweet. Every word she said was true. More women started chiming in, sharing not just "you go girl" cheesy sentiments, but thoughtful comments about what happens when women speak truth to power. I'm not comparing it to a #MeToo thing, because nothing about it smacked of victimhood. It was just smart women from all walks of life and classes discussing facts.

I think CBS would have preferred that I check into a nunnery under an assumed name until they were ready to finally air the damn thing. Every few days, Anderson Cooper would personally call me to say, "It's coming together." I think he was genuine, but I can also see someone suggesting that a call from him would make me feel better. When they said it was going to come out March 18, the day after my birthday, I was relieved.

Cohen then stated he would seek twenty million dollars from me, which he said was his tally of how many times I had talked. One million dollars for each "breach." *60 Minutes* pushed it one last time, to March 25. But now they wanted to do additional shooting of me at home for B-roll, the fluff day-in-the-life footage to keep viewers interested during boring narration.

I didn't want to do it and wasn't going to be in Texas anyway. I compromised, letting them film me at my dads' house in L.A. They filmed me with Keith's horses, even though they're not the right breeds to do what I do. It didn't look anything like Texas.

I couldn't believe they wanted this stuff. Then they shot what felt like two hours of me watering flowers.

Why were we wasting even a second with fluff when there was so much information to cram in? They shot a three-hour interview of me and Anderson—even if they gave me the whole episode without commercials, the show is literally called *60 Minutes*!

I watched the show live as it aired March 25. Anderson sat on a chair in front of a huge photo of me. "A week before the 2016 election, Donald Trump's personal attorney paid a porn star named Stormy Daniels to keep quiet about her alleged relationship with the Republican candidate for president. Today, that arrangement is well on its way to becoming the most talked-about 'hush agreement' in history. . . ."

I only know what he said because I watched it again. The first time I watched it, I was just staring at my photo, horrified by how bad I looked. My makeup was terrible. Here I was, finally getting my chance to talk, and I had to work through my feelings about vanity. That done, my thoughts turned to "I can't believe they used so little." Anderson had done such a fantastic job interviewing me, and there was so much focus on what happened in the hotel room in Lake Tahoe, and then in the parking lot in Las Vegas when my daughter and I were threatened. But as edited, the reasons behind my decisions, all the things that I have detailed for you here, seemed unclear. Still, more than twenty-one million people watched it, a bump of over 100 percent from the previous week's show. In fact, it was the most-watched episode since the November 2008 postelection interview with Barack and Michelle Obama. I bet Trump *really* hated to hear that.

I had some close friends, including Denver Nicks, over to watch the show with me as it aired, and Glen waited to go ballistic until it was over. At first I didn't understand and thought it was because it was so public.

"A man fucking threatened you and our daughter, Stormy," he said. "My daughter. And it never occurred to you to tell me. It never once crossed your mind that as a mother you should tell me someone threatened you."

"I forgot!"

"You forgot?" he said. "Stop lying to me."

"I have had so much shit going on, Glen," I said. "Yes, I forgot. He didn't kill me. I am sorry that I didn't tell you. I am so sorry any of this is happening."

"I asked you if there was anything else I should know and you lied to me."

"But you were not well," I said. "I was afraid to tell you anything."

He stormed out. My phone kept chiming, so I picked it up. I scrolled through my direct messages, and death threats were coming in. I got about a hundred. "Your child should be euthanized," read one, "because she would be better off than with you." So many threats involved people wanting to take my daughter away from me, one way or another.

Everyone left but Denver, and I asked him to do me a favor. "I need you to film me giving a statement," I said, asking him to get out his iPhone. I think he assumed he was taping me for some sort of clarification or response that I would then post on social media. No, this was personal.

"If something happens to me," I began, directly addressing my seven-year-old daughter, "I love you." I shared my hopes for her and my pride in the smart, funny, sweet girl I have had the privilege to raise. I told Glen I love him, and then I started reeling off a last will and testament, never so direct about anything in my life. I said who to contact about my life insurance policy, cautioning that the person should not immediately give the money to Glen. "He will be in a bad spot," I said. I talked about the care of my horses, stating that one of the horses should be sold and the money should be put into an account for my daughter. I cared about the living. Stuff didn't matter. I had the clear-eyed vision of a person about to die.

Throughout, Denver kept looking up, fully feeling the solemnity of the moment. When it was over, I nodded at him to turn off his camera, and he sat on the couch next to me with a heavy exhale. "What do you want me to do with this?" he asked.

"Put it on a thumb drive and don't say a word about where

it's at until I'm killed," I said. I was that certain. I told him who to give it to, and we haven't discussed it since. I had lived alone with the fear of being murdered to ensure my silence for so long that now that the world was discussing the death threats against me, I felt like I finally had some company in my concern. Dark humor is one of my coping mechanisms, and I often joke about it now. Sometime after we taped that final statement, I made the mistake of telling Denver that I had joined a celebrity deadpool, a death-watch list where you bet on the likelihood of a famous person dying that year. "I bet on myself," I told him.

"Stop it," he said.

"What?" I said. "It's funny."

"It's not funny, Stormy," he said. "This is a real thing."

"If it's not funny, it will be real," I said. "I need it to be funny or else my daughter isn't going to grow up with a mother. So let's go with funny. Funny works."

But I also needed to face the fact that I needed bodyguards. I am the Goldilocks of security teams. The first two guys I had just didn't work out. That very first night with them, Kayla and I were working and managed to give them the slip. It was childish to fuck with the babysitters, but it was also a test that I think they should have passed. The second pair was great, but I needed someone long-term. And the third was just right.

Brandon and Travis became my dragons. My code name is Daenerys, Mother of Dragons, from *Game of Thrones*. We were insta-family, and they are a team of equals. Brandon is stoic and analytical. I watch him watching everything in whatever public setting I go into, his eyes scanning the entire scene, taking in any anomaly and assessing if it's a danger. But he is also incredibly goofy. On long drives he'll be in the front seat doing the most dead-on but respectful Obama impression you've ever heard. Travis is more passionate, like me, always listening to his intuition. I call him my M&M with the hard shell and soft interior.

After the second night I was under their protection, they later told me they went back to their hotel room and sat there quiet for a moment. Travis recalled saying, "Are you going to say it or am I?" They agreed they were going to leave all their other clients and work with me full-time. I had been praying they would but was afraid they would feel obligated.

They knew I was going to New York for Michael Cohen's April 16 hearing in a federal courthouse about the documents the FBI seized from him. Michael Avenatti wanted me to be at the hearing in case I was needed. If the conversation isn't with you, it's just about you, right?

"Who's going to be with you in New York?" Travis asked me.

"I don't know," I said.

"We got you," said Brandon.

THIRTEEN

I was half dressed in the back of a speeding car in New York City, trying to zip up my skirt. My flight out of West Palm Beach—where I had had a dance booking—had been delayed, and there went all my plans to prep for Michael Cohen's April 16 court hearing. The FBI had raided his home, office, and hotel room on April 9 seeking information on, among other things, the $130,000 he paid me. The hearing was about who got to look at the seized documents—Trump's lawyers, who I would not trust to hold a Red Bull for me while I ran to the bathroom, or, as is more usual, a panel of prosecutors unrelated to the case. Michael and I wanted to be there because I am a firm believer that if someone is talking about me, they can say it to my face.

Now we just had to get there in time. My dragons, Brandon and Travis, hustled me right from the plane to the car. Glen wanted to come to the courthouse to stand by me, but I left him at the airport to wait for my checked bag. It was full of my dance costumes, the things I most care about after my people and horses. Thank God I had thought to roll up my court outfit in my carry-on.

I had lined up a hotel to go to before the hearing, so I could shower and steam-iron my skirt suit. It was lilac, sure to show every wrinkle. Now I didn't even have time to touch up my makeup. I just had to wear the remnants of the makeup from the night before and run my hands through my hair, limp and tired from the humidity of Florida.

If this wasn't enough of a shit show, there wasn't even time for me to go to the bathroom before getting in the car. There's no other way to say this: I was on my period and I desperately needed to change my tampon.

"Dude," I said to Travis, "the second we get in, I need to find a bathroom."

"Can you hold it?"

"It's not about holding it," I said.

This big giant of a man grimaced and whispered, "You have to do number two?"

"No," I said. "I have to do number three."

"What the—" he said. "Oh. Oh. I got you, girl."

We got to the federal courthouse on Pearl Street in downtown Manhattan and I could see there was a mob of photographers and press waiting. Travis and Brandon have a routine for getting me safely out of a car when there are a lot of people, but I had never been in something like this. "Wait," I yelled to Travis before he opened his door. I didn't want to carry my bag, and I didn't want to walk in like I was looking to be a feminine hygiene spokesmodel. "Here," I said, handing him the tampon. "Hold this in your jacket for me."

"You got it," he said.

"You ready for this?" Brandon asked.

"Nope," I said. "Let's go."

Michael Avenatti was suddenly there, just as the sea of men with cameras rushed toward us. I was unprepared for them being so close and able to jostle me. I thought because it was a legal building, there would be police and everyone would be cordoned off. They were pushing at the dragons, who were trying to keep me steady on my feet. I almost fell, and I was frightened. A man was screaming, "Stormy, are you here to rattle Michael Cohen? Stormy, are you here to rattle Michael Cohen?"

I got inside, and they just pressed up against the glass, watching me as I went through the metal detector. I didn't realize I was shaking until Brandon put his hand on my back to steady me. I could hear a woman scream outside, like it was a rock concert, "Stormy, we love you!"

We were told the courtroom door would be closing soon, so we raced. No time for a bathroom. I have to face Cohen and all I'm thinking about is *Is my tampon gonna hold*? I was wearing this light skirt, and that was what would be all over the front page the next day. STORMY DANIELS, SHOT IN THE ASS. *Tragic.* People would think I did it on purpose for attention.

We got to the doors just in time and a guard stopped us. "You can't go in," he said. "It's full."

"Excuse me, what?" I said.

Michael asserted himself. He doesn't like to be told no or be embarrassed. The guy went away for a minute, then came back. "I have to bring someone to bring some chairs in," he said. "You can't walk in and stand. You're going to be in folding chairs in the back of the gallery. Give me five minutes."

Five minutes. "I'm going to the bathroom," I said.

I started walking, and Travis opened his suit jacket and

handed me the tampon in a high-five gesture. It was the perfect handoff. Tampon, check. I did my female thing and came back with seconds to spare.

The doors opened, and I stayed stoic as I took my seat. Cohen was already there, sitting at what would be the defendant's table if this were a trial. Every single head but his turned to register my appearance. He didn't look at me once.

The Honorable Kimba Wood entered the courtroom. At seventy-four, she'd been a judge for nearly thirty years, having been appointed to the bench by Ronald Reagan. I had done some googling on her and liked her. When she was young she went to the London School of Economics, and she took a job at Hugh Hefner's Playboy Casino. She quit after six days of training as a croupier. Hey, if you don't want to be a Playboy bunny, be a federal judge. American women deserve to have choices.

I had heard she was annoyed at Friday's hearing, three days before, because Cohen hadn't shown up. He was too busy smoking cigars with cronies—and paparazzi—in Midtown, the buffoon playing the part of the Mafia-movie tough guy. Judge Wood had said Friday that she needed to know who Cohen's clients were by Monday morning. His lawyers said he had just three.

Now, we already knew two of them: President Trump, obviously, and a Republican fund-raiser and lobbyist named Elliott Broidy. After the election, Trump named Broidy deputy national finance chairman for the Republican National Committee—a title that Cohen shared. I knew that Cohen dealt with *Playboy* model Shera Bechard's signing of an NDA about an affair with a man who got her pregnant, a man whose alias in the hush agreement will ring a bell: David Dennison. The same name Cohen chose for Trump in *my* NDA. Hunh. Shera even got my alias, Peggy Peterson. That Friday, *The Wall Street Journal* reported that Cohen helped Broidy negotiate a payoff of $1.6 million to Bechard through Cohen's shell company Essential Consultants LLC to, guess who, my ex-lawyer Keith Davidson. When reached for comment by *The New York Times,* Broidy sure copped to Trump being the guy fast. In the *Times,* Shera's *new* lawyer, Peter K. Stris, also accused Cohen and Davidson of working against his client's interests, or, as he put it, "profoundly disturbing and repeated collusion." Both men have denied this.

But who was bachelor number three? One of Cohen's lawyers told Judge Wood that he had consulted the third client over the weekend and the person didn't want his name out there.

"At this point, no one would want to be associated with the case in that way," said the lawyer, and I had to stop myself from yelling, "No shit!" But Wood wasn't having it and demanded that the lawyer reveal the name.

"Your honor, the client's name that is involved is Sean Hannity," he said.

There was this eruption of gasps and do-you-believe-this chuckles in the courtroom, like a big reveal in a comic film. The Fox News know-it-all and Trump BFF was tied up with Cohen. (Right away, Hannity took to Twitter to deny Cohen ever represented him. That night on his show he had this hysterical take on the legal system: "Never paid him any fees," he said. "I might have handed him ten bucks. 'I definitely want attorney-client privilege on this.' Something like that.")

After that big *Legally Blonde* moment in the courtroom, it was kind of boring, to be honest. It just went on and on for three hours, with the lawyers saying the same thing over and over. I was very aware that my stomach was growling loud enough for people to hear, but at least I wasn't bleeding all over the place.

The best part was that the world was finally seeing what I knew. They thought Michael Cohen was this mastermind, a consigliere who fixed everything. No, he's a complete fucking moron. The world would not know anything about me without him constantly getting in his own way.

The sea of photographers was still raging when we walked out of the courthouse, but now there was a little island of sidewalk to stand on and make my statement. I went up to what looked like a tangled bouquet of fifteen microphones and leaned in. "Hi, everyone," I said. The crowd noise was so loud that I couldn't hear myself. But I had to get past my nerves. I was finally getting to speak without a filter.

"So, for years Mr. Cohen has acted like he is above the law," I began. "He has considered himself and openly referred to himself as Mr. Trump's fixer. He has played by a different set of rules, or should I say, no rules at all. He has never thought that the little man or especially woman—and even more, women like me—mattered. That ends now. My attorney and I are committed to making sure that everyone finds out the truth and the facts of what happened. And I give my word that we will not rest until that happens. Thank you."

I looked at Michael, who was standing to my left. I gave him a look of *Was that good?* He suppressed a smile. I had said what I came to say, and I was just getting started.

The next morning, Brandon and Travis whisked me into the ABC Television Center for the April 17 live taping of *The View.*

After *60 Minutes,* I was determined to do my own makeup and told the producers so. When I met the ladies, everyone was very nice. But when I went to shake the hand of Meghan McCain, I could tell by the way she did it that she did *not* want to have to touch me. She clearly despised me. Meghan is the resident conservative, and right before the show I could tell people were super worried that she was going to say something that offended me.

I thought that if she had something to say that wasn't a vicious attack, then she should say it. And I'm not lying, so I have no problem answering anything. I hoped she would.

I sat backstage watching the beginning of the show, with the announcer talking up my appearance and calling me "the woman everyone in America is talking about." Right away, Whoopi Goldberg turned the focus to Meghan, asking for an update on the condition of her father, Senator John McCain. The senator had to have emergency surgery for complications in his treatment for brain cancer. "I had a really rough morning," Meghan said, announcing that she would soon be going to be with him in Arizona. She added that her father would be watching the show. Now I really wanted her to ask me whatever question was weighing on her heart.

After the first commercial break, they sat me in the middle of the table, with Michael sitting to my left. Joy Behar asked me why I came there knowing I was under the threat of President Trump suing me for twenty million dollars if I talked. "I'm tired of being threatened," I said. "I'm done being bullied. I'm done."

"Will you have to pay the twenty million?" she asked.

"I'd have to get twenty million first," I answered. The crowd roared. I smiled. Meghan didn't.

They asked why I attended Michael Cohen's court hearing. I said I wasn't sure if they were going to be discussing my case, and I wanted to be prepared.

Meghan paused for a second before going in. "It seems like a publicity stunt on some level," she started. *Good girl,* I thought. *Say what you want.* She finished with "I hadn't heard your name until all this happened and now you are literally live on *The View* giving an entire interview to us."

I was grateful she gave me the opportunity to talk about this. "This isn't what I want to be known for," I said. "As a matter of fact, I hid for quite a while, and it's overwhelming and intimidating and downright scary sometimes." I mentioned the cost to my family, but also the literal cost of bodyguards. "You don't want to know their food bill, because I have to feed them three times a day and they are big." My dragons hated that and made me feel guilty about it for weeks!

When Joy tried to deflect the question, I returned my attention to Meghan. "Meghan has a very, very good question, and if I were her or anyone else, that's what I would be saying. A lot of people have."

I liked that she grew some balls and asked it. Especially with her war-hero dad watching at home. I have crazy respect for her, because up until then I thought maybe she was just going to be all bark. Afterward, people brought it up to me, saying things like "She should have kept her mouth shut. You were a guest in her house."

No. She wanted to know the answer to something that bothered her, she was told not to, and she did it anyway. I gave her my answer, and she listened. She sat there, open-minded, and she was a big enough person to accept my answer.

When it was over, she shook my hand again and this time there was a mutual respect, if not regard.

"Maybe you'll come back," she said.

"I would like that," I said, meaning it. I appreciate that the other women were so kind to me, but I knew they supported me from the beginning. Either because they understood the law of the case or had a natural sympathy for anyone standing up to Trump. Meghan I had to win over. I don't think I changed her opinion of me wholly, and I definitely don't think I changed her opinion of porn. All I care about is that she wouldn't allow herself to be silenced.

When I go back, I am most excited to see her again. Maybe she'll change *my* mind about something.

President Trump must have been watching along with Senator McCain, because he broke his Twitter silence about me. We do know he loves his TV time. On the show, Michael and I presented a sketch of the man who threatened my daughter and me in the Las Vegas parking lot. "A sketch years later about a nonexistent man," he tweeted at six in the morning on April 18, probably from the toilet. "A total con job, playing the Fake News Media for Fools (but they know it)!"

Never mind that the sketch was done by renowned forensic artist Lois Gibson, whose sketches have helped law enforcement ID 751 criminals and secure more than a thousand convictions. Lois has said she was inspired to study forensic art after she was attacked at age twenty-one by a brutal rapist. He almost killed her, repeatedly strangling her until she passed out, laughing each time. Back then, she was a model and dancer in L.A., and she was afraid to go to the police. Just the kind of person Trump and

Cohen would write off. But Lois and I believe in each other, because honest people can spot honest people. And liars.

Two weeks after Trump said I was running a "con job," Michael Avenatti filed a defamation lawsuit against him. "Mr. Trump knew that his false, disparaging statement would be read by people around the world," Michael wrote in the lawsuit, "as well as widely reported, and that Ms. Clifford would be subjected to threats of violence, economic harm, and reputational damage as a result." Translation from legalese: If you come for us, we're ready.

People have been coming for poor Michael in more inventive ways. Ever since he's been on TV, he's had all these people sending him naked pictures—hundreds of pictures. Of all types of women. He's anything but stupid, and we both think they're setups to get him in a room to say he was a john or accuse him of assault. We were talking on the phone while he was in L.A., and I made him screen-shot one for me.

When I saw the picture, I immediately recognized the girl as a porn star from the UK. Despite the fact that the girl had sent him an unsolicited message saying she lives in Woodland Hills, giving him an address and trying to lure him to "come over."

We both agreed that everywhere you turn in this case, someone is trying to fuck us over.

FOURTEEN

We were getting ready to land when the flight attendant passed me the folded note. He looked at me and nodded, then left before I could open it. In blue ink, he had written the words "Stay Strong." He had perfect timing, because I had just read the most horrible, untrue thing about myself, the latest in a series, and I needed that lifeline. For some time, I had felt like I was caught in a tornado. I was swirling in this mess, at the mercy of every news alert, think piece, hot take, and court filing. I used to click all the stories about the case, but then I would get all bent out of shape over stuff that wasn't from a legit source. Which I think describes a lot of us.

So I stopped reading about Stormy Daniels and focused on being Stormy Daniels. Besides, I was busy. People all over the country want to pay me more to do the shows that I have always loved doing. People might criticize that, but why am I not allowed to honor that great tenet of American capitalism: supply and demand? With my schedule, most of the world finds out about developments in my case at least half a day before I do. On April 27, two days after Michael Cohen pleaded the fifth in my lawsuit saying the NDA was null and void, a judge granted him a three-month postponement in my civil case because, as

His Honor put it, Cohen will "likely" be indicted in a criminal case. The media jumped on it and talked about it all day, but I didn't know until I was sitting in my makeshift dressing room, the manager's office of Fantasies strip club in Baltimore. I was half dressed between shows, my feet up as I finally got around to Michael's emails of the day. I trust Michael as an advocate for me, and I am no longer on my own.

I needed breaks from engaging in the national conversation about me, so I relied on the small, personal encounters I had meeting people in clubs across the country. I have been writing all of this to you in the mornings on the road, waking up in hotels, or on my tour bus. I write before anyone in the circus wakes up: my two dragons, Brandon and Travis; and Denver, who I am grateful for dropping out of his life in New York to give me the day-to-day normalcy of always having a true friend around. And now there's Dwayne, my old roadie from years ago. A couple of months ago, something told me to call him. "Hey, do you want to be my tour manager?"

"I just started this really good-paying job at a sound company," he said. "Let me talk to my wife." He called me the next day.

"I'm in," he said, and after a brief pause, added, "Are you gonna pay me?" He told me he felt like he was just supposed to come along. We picked up sweet Chris, my emcee, at my gig at Country Rock Cabaret in St. Louis. He just seemed so capable that, again, I had the voice telling me to bring him along. "You're coming with me," I said.

And he joked in a hypnotized voice, "I'm coming with you." He is one of the most gifted emcees out there. Give him a mic and he will announce your arrival and pump up the crowd like you invented stripping. The guys are all so different, but they're brothers now.

At my meet-and-greets after shows, Travis and Brandon stand beside me as the person hands either Chris or Dwayne their cell phone to take a picture. They all hear the stories people confide in me. Men and, especially now, women take those minutes to tell me about their lives and how they identify with me. As I've said, they tell me they need me to save the world.

It's a burden to take in all this energy, but I know it's what I am supposed to be doing. There were so many times that the universe took care of me—times where I should not have done well, shouldn't have gotten out of a situation, or shouldn't have risen above because no one helped me. You've seen this time and again in these pages: the universe takes my hand and says, "I got you." And I think it wants its payback.

I decided I would do one more big media thing, but only because it felt like family to me. *Saturday Night Live,* my favorite show in the world, asked me to take part in the cold open of the May 5 episode. There was talk of it for a few weeks, and then, just a few days beforehand, I got word that it was a go. They wanted to do a huge cold open, an old-fashioned cavalcade of stars, with all these unexpected stars playing the roles of people caught up in the various scandals of the Trump administration.

They wanted me to be the last and biggest surprise, and kept my appearance so top secret that they didn't tell any of the cast beforehand. I entered 30 Rock through an underground parking entrance and was so busy pinching myself that I almost ran right into Scarlett Johansson as we both boarded the building's secret elevator. She was there to play Ivanka Trump, and Jimmy Fallon would be Jared Kushner. Upstairs, I was spirited to my dressing room, right next door to Ben Stiller's. He was perfectly cast as Michael Cohen, calling everyone on his various burner phones. As word got out that I was there, cast members kept stopping by to take selfies with me. I couldn't believe these people I admired were losing it that I was there. I only had a few minutes with my favorite, Kate McKinnon, because she had to do heavy-duty makeup to play crypt keeper Rudy Giuliani. But my other absolute favorite, Leslie Jones, was able to talk to me for a while. In the hallway, I hugged Ben Stiller, and we got to talking about how much we preferred directing over acting. *Um, hello,* I thought in the moment, *I am talking to Ben Stiller about directing* Tropic Thunder *and* Zoolander.

Alec Baldwin walked in, and I made a funny face at the absurdity of him dressed as Donald Trump. He'd brought his wife, Hilaria, who at any moment would be giving birth to their baby boy. He was just as charming as you want him to be. But the real surprise was Lorne Michaels. He'd left a note with flowers in my dressing room, but he also stopped by. I don't get starstruck, but I have known this man all my life through watching *SNL,* the show he created in 1975. All those nights I stayed up late in Baton Rouge, or, later, watching it Sunday morning after taping it because I had a Saturday night show. I tried not to gush or give off the feel of crazy-stalker fan, but I did tell him this was my dream come true. He invited me to sit with him in his special spot in the bleachers once the cold open was finished.

Once the show started, each reveal got a cheer, and I almost broke character when I got the biggest wave of surprised applause.

As Trump, Alec dismisses Cohen and tries to sweet-talk me. "Oh, come on, we'll always have Shark Week," he said. "I solved North and South Korea, why can't I solve us?"

"Sorry, Donald, it's too late for that," I said. "I know you don't believe in climate change, but . . . a storm's a-coming, baby!"

And then we got to say those magic words together: "Live from New York, it's *Saturday Night!*"

I went and sat with Lorne to watch the host, Donald Glover, and for me, the second show was watching Lorne in action. It was amazing to see somebody of his stature still be so involved in every bit of the process, exactly how I try to be as a director.

When the show was over, we all gathered on the stage to say good night to the audience, just as I had seen over and over again. The girl from Baton Rouge who wasn't going to amount to anything was standing up there just like she'd imagined. When I stepped off the stage, I had a realization: that was the best thing that had ever happened to me besides having a child. The only thing that could ever top it would be having another baby—and that was not happening.

"What do I do now?" I said, back in the car with my bodyguards, Travis and Brandon, on our way to the after-party. "Should I, like, buy a puppy or something?"

Then there are moments where I am back down on earth. This was all so hard on my marriage. For months, Glen became more and more critical of me, saying I was being dramatic about needing security. He got a sense of what it's like when I went home for Mother's Day weekend. I gave my dragons the day off, and on a whim, Glen and I went to the May 11 Lynyrd Skynyrd concert at the Dos Equis Pavilion, this huge outdoor amphitheater in Dallas. Bad Company was opening for them and were already playing when we got there slightly late. It was an old-fashioned date night, the kind women's magazines always tell you to have to save your marriage. We were in the third row, Paul Rodgers was singing "Feel Like Making Love," and Glen hugged me, just like he did when I fell in love with him watching Snow Patrol sing "Chasing Cars" more than ten years before.

Then Bad Company left the stage. And the lights came on, and people saw me. This girl leaned over. "Hey, can I get a picture with you?" she whispered. "I'm a big fan. Do you mind if I just get a quick selfie with you?"

Glen looked away. I smiled. "Sure," I said. She did, and that's all anyone else had to hear. They descended on us. "Can I get a picture?" "Can I get a picture?" People began pulling at me, guys putting their arms over me to get me into the frame of their cameras. Glen started to block people, but they were coming from all sides. Someone ripped my shirt trying to grab me, and Glen was done. We fled to the parking lot and sat in the car. No one chased us, it wasn't some zombie apocalypse thing, but when I was in that space, people wanted a piece of me.

I was used to it and blamed myself for thinking I could just do something like this without Brandon and Travis. But Glen had never seen anything like it. In the car, he admitted it was downright scary, comparing it to *Finding Nemo,* when the seagulls are all coming for the crab, saying, "Mine. Mine. Mine."

I was relieved he saw it up close. "That's what it's been like," I told him, not saying what I wanted to say: "I told you I wasn't exaggerating."

Still, I didn't want the night to be a wash. When we heard Lynyrd Skynyrd start up, we sneaked back in, safe again in the dark. We left halfway through "Free Bird," walking away as they sang about someone who would rather be alone than be chained.

I was in Raleigh on June 7, in the middle of a two-night run at the Men's Club. My phone was buzzing with messages that morning, but I chose to ignore it because an equestrian center run by a horse friend of mine had opened early just for me. With no cameras, and nobody watching except my kindred-spirit crazy-wonderful horse folk, I got to ride again. It felt amazing to be that free.

When I get a ton of texts, it usually means I am being talked about in the media. For my sanity, I just sort of peek quick to get the gist. If it's important, Denver or Michael will tell me. That morning I was getting random Facebook messages of support and apologies for what Trump's pal and lawyer Rudy Giuliani said about me. I didn't want to look, but a girlfriend sent me the text of his speech with the subject "Fuck Rudy." He attacked my integrity during a speech in Tel Aviv the day before. "I'm sorry, I don't respect a porn star the way I respect a career woman or a woman of substance or a woman who has great respect for herself as a woman and as a person and isn't going to sell her body for sexual exploitation. . . . I mean, she has no reputation. If you're going to sell your body for money, you just don't have a reputation."

So all day I'll be a talking point about how we value women in society. Who gets to be believed. I'd rather they talk about the lawsuit we filed the day before against Michael Cohen and Keith Davidson. We have seventeen texts between them. Michael Avenatti emailed me the texts in a document.

I put off reading them for a while, knowing it would just start a round of me pacing and cussing. But finally, I made myself do it. On January 17, the day *In Touch* published my 2011 interview, Cohen texted Davidson, desperate to get me to go on *The Sean*

Hannity Show to discredit the story live on the air. "I have her tentatively scheduled for Hannity tonight," Cohen wrote in an iMessage. Then there are all these texts back and forth. Meanwhile, my life was falling apart and Glen was screaming at me.

Davidson tells Cohen he couldn't get me to do it and says he can try for tomorrow. Cohen writes back: "Let's forget tonight. They [Fox news and the Trump administration] would rather tomorrow so they can promote the heck out of the show." (His brackets, not mine!)

Two hours later, Cohen messaged Davidson about Trump's strategy again. "Keith, the wise men all believe the story is dying and don't think it's smart for her to do any interviews. Let her do her thing but no interviews at all with anyone."

A minute later, Davidson—who was supposed to be my attorney—responded, "One hundred percent."

"Thanks pal," wrote Cohen, quickly adding, "Just no interviews or statements unless through you."

"Got it," Davidson responded.

I was devastated. The text conversation seemed to justify all the doubts and fears I'd felt while Davidson was representing me. Although it's for the court to make a legal decision on what the texts mean, in the context of any other evidence produced, reading them now validated my sense of betrayal. Michael had evidence, too, that when I finally fired Davidson, he tipped off Cohen immediately that I was going to share my story.

The wise men were wrong about the story dying. Maybe they should have asked a wise woman. It never occurred to any of these men that I would someday have a voice.

EPILOGUE

Though my book has to end somewhere, my story goes on. The last month has been as eventful as any that came before it.

In July, I was arrested while performing at a strip club in Columbus, Ohio, in what seems to have been a sting operation orchestrated by a pro-Trump detective. The bogus charges were dropped first thing the next morning, but only after I endured hours in painfully tight handcuffs and spent the night in jail.

Reports of the whole scary episode instantly made headlines. With police body cam footage of me getting hauled away in handcuffs splashed across television news, Glen reached his breaking point and began making preparations to file for divorce. Days later, he emptied our bank account, disappeared in the car with our daughter, and filed a temporary restraining order against me that prevented me from coming near her. I had the agonizing experience of reading about the restraining order and my divorce papers, which were full of disgusting and completely false claims, on a gossip site.

I'd stopped wearing my wedding band months earlier and we had discussed ending our marriage for a long time, but what Glen did still came as a massive shock. I was devastated. I had almost no money, the car was gone, I had no idea where my daughter was, and I was forbidden by law from even talking to her on the phone.

Those terrifying days after Glen vanished with our daughter and threatened to keep her from me forever were the darkest days of my life. The whole reason for everything I had done—to protect my family—was suddenly blowing up in my face. Glen was hurt, angry, and afraid, and what he did in that moment I know he thought was right, but it's still difficult to square with the man I fell in love with. I guess it's a testament to just how painful and stressful 2018 has been for my family, since the news broke of a brief tryst I had more than a decade ago with a goofy reality TV star who now lives at 1600 Pennsylvania Avenue.

Thankfully, once the dust settled, Glen and I were able to come together and let our love for our daughter and for each other be our guide as we made more fair and sensible arrangements for ending our marriage. He dropped the restraining order nonsense, returned the car, and we've agreed to share custody of our beautiful little girl. We may not be a married couple any longer, but we'll always be her parents.

Where does my story go from here? I can't say I know, but I'm excited to see what comes next. I can look back on a life more full and certainly more interesting than I, as a little girl back in Baton Rouge just trying to survive and spend time with my horses, ever thought it would be. This most recent chapter has been quite the adventure, with ups and downs, new friendships formed, and old relationships lost. But as exciting and trying as things are right now, I know it won't always be like this. As a friend of mine keeps reminding me, nothing lasts forever.